INTERNATIONAL LAW
TODAY AND TOMORROW

INTERNATIONAL LAW
TODAY AND TOMORROW

by

OLIVER J. LISSITZYN

Published for the
PARKER SCHOOL OF FOREIGN AND COMPARATIVE LAW
Columbia University in the City of New York
by
OCEANA PUBLICATIONS, INC.
DOBBS FERRY, NEW YORK
1965

© Copyright 1965 by Oliver J. Lissitzyn

Library of Congress Catalog Card No. 65-22165

MANUFACTURED IN THE UNITED STATES OF AMERICA

PREFATORY NOTE

A part of this study first appeared in *International Conciliation* (March 1963) under the title "International Law in a Divided World." The author is grateful to the officers and staff of the Carnegie Endowment for International Peace for encouraging him to prepare this thoroughly revised and much enlarged version of the original essay. An entirely new section on "The Nature and Content of International Law" has been added and an extensive bibliography has been appended.

Oliver J. Lissitzyn

June 1965.

CONTENTS

FOREWORD

Professor Lissitzyn's "International Law in a Divided World" was first published by the Carnegie Endowment in the March 1963 issue of *International Conciliation*. The intrinsic merit of this scholarly assessment of the role and function of international law in the modern world is perhaps best attested by its reception. In the brief span since it appeared, it has become something of a classic in English-speaking countries; an Arabic version has already been published and French and Spanish editions will appear shortly. The Endowment is proud to have been instrumental in the publication of Professor Lissitzyn's article, and gratified that he has expanded it in the present volume.

Since the end of World War II, one often hears about a crisis in international law. It is, of course, true that international law has been subject to challenge and attacks from various quarters. It is also true that, despite much talk of peaceful settlement of international disputes and peaceful co-existence, members of the international community rarely submit their disputes to impartial third-party adjudication either by the International Court of Justice or by Arbitral Tribunals. It is further true that since 1945, there has been a series of major crises in various parts of the world for most of which there is no purely legal solution. But there is nothing new in this. At most it is no more than an intensification of tendencies or attitudes that have long been manifest. In any case, it is certainly an exaggeration to speak about a current crisis in international law. What we see in fact is the evolution and expansion of international law and its progressive development as it struggles to adjust itself to a world that is in continuous and indeed revolutionary transformation. What are characterized as crises could perhaps more aptly be de-

ix

scribed as the growing pains of the admittedly primitive system of international law. Rather than despair, we should be encouraged by its significant expansion into new areas and by widespread and sustained efforts to clarify uncertainties and to resolve conflicting interpretations.

Professor Lissitzyn's study puts the role and function, the limits and the potentialities of international law into proper perspective. Scholars everywhere will welcome this truly significant contribution to contemporary literature on international law, and others who are concerned for the progress toward peace will find in it much that bears directly on their concern.

JOSEPH E. JOHNSON

"IN PARTES TRES"

MORE THAN FIFTY YEARS AGO, echoing the optimism of the nineteenth century, the author of a standard British treatise on international law confidently asserted that "immeasurable progress is guaranteed to International Law, since there are eternal moral and economic factors working in its favour."[1] Today many Western jurists are asking, with varying degrees of pessimism, whether or not there is still something that can be properly called universal international law, and, if so, whether or not the universality of international law can long be maintained in the face of the cold war and the rise to statehood of an ever growing number of nations of non-Western antecedents.

As early as the inter-war period, some Western jurists saw a threat to international law in the rejection by the rulers of the Soviet Union of the fundamental values and premises of Western public order. At that time the Soviet Union was hardly strong enough to defy the West, and the Soviet challenge to international law was soon overshadowed by that of the aggressive nihilism of the Axis powers, particularly Nazi Germany. The emergence of the Soviet Union after World War II as one of the superpowers, however, could not but increase the anxiety of Western observers, some of whom saw in the resulting "disunity" of mankind a threat to the very existence of international law.[2]

The fear that the appearance of newly independent nations in Asia and Africa would destroy the universality of

[1] L. Oppenheim, *International Law: A Treatise* (2nd ed., London, Longmans, Green, 1912), Vol. 1, p. 83.

[2] See, for example, H. A. Smith, *The Crisis in the Law of Nations* (London, Stevens, 1947), pp. 17-32, 101, and *passim; cf.* M. S. McDougal *et al., Studies in World Public Order* (New Haven, Yale Univ. Press, 1960), pp. 988-989; K. Wilk, "International Law and Global Ideological Conflict," *American Journal of International Law (AJIL)*, Vol. 45, No. 4 (Oct. 1951), p. 648.

1

international law has been based partly on the notion that international law, created and nurtured in the culture of the West, cannot be fully understood and wholeheartedly accepted as a guide to conduct by nations whose cultural heritage is not Western. There is also apprehension that the newly independent states, together with other less developed nations, may be disinclined to accept certain norms, developed mainly by the more advanced and stronger states of the West, that have served to protect Western public and private interests. The "expansion" of international law in Asian and African nations is said to be proceeding at the price of a "continuous dilution of its content, as it is reinterpreted for the benefit of the newcomers."[3]

That the world is roughly divided today into three parts —the Communist states, the more advanced nations of the West, and the less developed countries—cannot be denied. But the division between the second and the third parts, drawn in terms of levels of economic development, does not correspond to distinctions of cultural background and recency of emancipation from colonial rule. Latin American nations are not highly developed economically, but share the Western cultural heritage and have been, for the most part, politically independent for more than a century. Japan, on the other hand, has a cultural background quite different from that of the West, but is highly developed economically and enjoyed, prior to World War II, great-power status. Before trying to appraise the impact of this tripartite division on international law and its universality, it is well to recall the origins of international law, its functions, and its traditional content.

---

[3] J. Stone, *Quest for Survival; The Role of Law and Foreign Policy* (Cambridge, Mass., Harvard Univ. Press, 1961), p. 88.

INTERNATIONAL LAW IN RETROSPECT

As a consciously recognized and practiced system of norms of interstate conduct deemed to be legally binding, international law is a product of modern Western civilization. Although in other ages and cultures some similar norms existed, they were not regarded as being susceptible of interpretation and application by legal methods. The unique role of the West in the development of international law was associated with the peculiarly western European interaction of several historical factors. Among these factors were the decline of the authority of religion, the rise of relatively small nation-states in a balance-of-power system, exploration and conquest of distant lands, revival of the study of Roman law, and the "law habit" which had developed in the pluralistic feudal society, partly under the influence of the Roman legal tradition. Two other factors were more fundamental: an increasingly productive and complex economy based on technological innovation, and the growing emphasis—related to the rise of science—on rational thought and action, with consequent growth of the ability to subordinate short-range advantages and emotional impulses to long-range considerations. The two came together and were probably inseparable.

International law appeared and grew because it served the needs of the society that was developing in the West. Without a minimum of order, predictability, and stability, the private economic activity of modern society could hardly be carried on. On a continent divided into many small states and increasingly dependent on distant lands for supplies and markets, domestic law alone could not provide the necessary modicum of security. There was a need for standards of official conduct that would be recognized and normally followed by all governments. Without such standards, the move-

3

ment of people, goods, and capital beyond national borders might be prohibitively risky. International law, furthermore, served to prevent unnecessary friction between governments and irrational destruction of values and resources.

Large parts of the traditional law of nations—including norms delimiting the sovereignty and jurisdiction of states, the law of the sea, the norms of treatment of foreign nationals, and much of the law of war and neutrality—directly served all these functions. Other parts of international law, including diplomatic immunities and the law of treaties, indirectly served the same functions by facilitating contacts and the conclusion of agreements between governments. The law of treaties eventually became the legal foundation of international organizations with all their manifold functions. Treaties have become the principal means of creating new norms which are regarded as binding on the states that accept them and of entrusting rule-making powers to international organs.

International law has also been used as an instrument of policy, either of cooperation or of conflict. It has served as a set of standards to which states appealed in disputes or conflicts of interest with other states, not only to persuade the other parties (or the arbitrators) to settle the conflicts in certain ways, but also as a symbol of rectitude to create or strengthen a consensus favorable to one of the parties and unfavorable to its opponents. This use of the law is not new. It may be recalled that the work of Grotius on the freedom of the seas, published in 1609, was written as a plea on behalf of a view of the law of the sea favorable to Dutch interests.

Scope and Effectiveness

Although general international law, that is, the norms regarded as binding on all members of the international community, has been an essential institution in the West, until the twentieth century the scope of its content and

4

authority was severely limited. Vast areas of discretion were left to the individual states. In the absence of restraints imposed by a treaty, a state had almost unlimited legal freedom to control its foreign trade and the movement of persons across its borders, although transnational economic activity was facilitated by norms that protected the citizen of a state and his property once he entered another state. International law purported to regulate the conduct of war, but the medieval attempt to distinguish just from unjust wars was given up and, subject to treaty restraints, every state was legally free to go to war with another state whenever its policy so dictated. This trait of international law distinguished it sharply from national legal systems in which both the preservation of public order and the prevention of private violence are generally regarded as among the most important functions of the law. Furthermore, although international law provided a set of standards to be applied by arbitrators, every state remained free, in the absence of an express undertaking to the contrary, to refuse to submit a dispute with another state to third-party settlement.

The very limitations on the sphere of operation of general international law made for its effectiveness. Since to a very large extent it did not purport to regulate the means by which a state could protect its major interests, it was generally not subjected to great strains. Furthermore, the stronger powers, at least in so far as they had common interests, had a preponderant influence on the development of its content and were not restrained from the use of force to repress what they regarded as violations of the law by others. International legal norms underwent constant reinterpretation and development—generally keeping in step with the evolving needs and policies of the stronger states. International law was thus fairly well adjusted to the realities of power and interest.

Nevertheless, no nation placed an absolute or overriding value on the observance of the law; it sometimes had to give way to other values, particularly in times of crisis. Further-

5

more, the universality of international law was never absolute. By definition, general international law was binding on all states. But quite aside from the fact that during much of the nineteenth century the participation of nations of non-European cultures in the international legal community was denied by many Western jurists, the Western community itself did not fully agree on many norms. For example, there were important and long-standing differences between British and Continental doctrines of prize law. The attempt to reconcile these doctrines in the Declaration of London of 1909 failed when Great Britain refused to ratify the Declaration. For many decades the United States upheld the novel "doctrine of voluntary expatriation," asserting that an individual who was voluntarily naturalized automatically lost his previous nationality even if the state of the latter continued to claim him as a subject. This doctrine was generally rejected in Europe and was not accepted at the Hague Conference for the Codification of International Law in 1930. In these examples and in many other cases, the doctrinal differences were caused, not by any diversity of cultural heritage, but by obvious divergences of national interest. There were no standing international courts to refine and unify the law through the adjudication of disputes.

Much of international law, moreover, was "particular" rather than "general." Many Latin American jurists believed in the existence of a regional law in Latin America based on distinctive principles and practices, such as diplomatic asylum and the doctrine of *uti possidetis*,[4] although they never denied that general international law also applied to American states. Of greater importance was the growing number of multilateral and bilateral treaties which contained detailed rules governing the conduct of the parties in relation to certain transnational activities and interests, but which were

---

[4] *I.e.*, the principle that boundaries between Spanish American nations should correspond to those between the political subdivisions of the Spanish colonial empire. See, in general, J. C. Puig, *Les Principes du Droit International Public Américain* (Paris, A. Pedone, 1954).

not binding on all states. The "particular" international law thus created by treaty could be visualized as consisting of a vast and ever changing number of circles of different and often fluctuating sizes, each enclosing a special "legal community" composed of the parties to a treaty.

Uncertainties and violations were not great enough to destroy the conviction of Western policy-making elites that international law, imperfect as it was, was an institution worthy of retention and development. The nineteenth-century European community of nations rested on a similarity of interests, values, and institutions, including those of private property and private enterprise on which the economic life of the community was based. The community operated within a framework of balance of power in which no one state could for long threaten the existence of the rest, and no member normally felt an interest in promoting basic changes or desired the destruction of the community itself. The resulting feeling of stability permitted appreciation of the long-range advantages of abiding by international law.

THE NATURE AND CONTENT
OF INTERNATIONAL LAW

"Law of Nations or International Law . . . is the name for the body of customary and conventional rules which are considered legally binding by civilized States in their intercourse with each other." [5] This opening statement in Oppenheim's treatise correctly summed up the conception of the nature and scope of public international law which was dominant during its classical era—from 1815 to World War I. This conception has lingered on and continues to exert considerable influence. Before attempting to appraise its adequacy today, it is well to consider in broad outline the content and functions of the main norms of international law as traditionally understood.[6]

States and Governments

Independent states—the entities which have developed modern international law—remain the most important centers of power and of formation of policy in the contemporary world. An independent state is a territorial entity with a permanent population governed by a central authority which maintains official relations with other similar entities and is not legally subject to control by any other such entity, although it recognizes the binding force of international law. Freedom from formal external control, capacity to enter into relations with other states, and the exercise of supreme authority within its territory, constitute the sovereignty of a

---

[5] Oppenheim, *op. cit.*, p. 3.

[6] In this study, the term "international law" is used in the sense of public international law. Private international law regulates the choice of law and other problems arising in national courts in litigation involving transnational elements of private-law nature.

state. Sovereignty, however, is never absolute. It is limited by international law, including all the treaties and agreements into which the state enters. No state denies the binding force of international law or refrains from official relations with at least some of the other states. No state wholly refrains from consenting to be bound by treaties and agreements.

General international law is by definition applicable to all independent states. In this sense, all independent states are equal. All independent states, moreover, are equally entitled to the protection of such rights and privileges as they have. But no two states have exactly the same totality of rights and duties under international law. This ensues from the fact that no two states have exactly the same treaty relations with other states. A state which has by treaty accorded to another state a right or privilege to which all states are not entitled by general international law has no duty to accord the same right or privilege to any other state unless it has undertaken to do so. Some states, moreover, may be bound by customary norms which are particular rather than general, that is, applicable to some but not all states.[7] And every state has the power "to dispose of its rights," that is, to give up its claims including those it may have under general international law. It may even consent to give up or limit its capacity to enter into diplomatic or treaty relations with other states, or to delegate the exercise of this capacity to another state. A state may thus be a party to a treaty concluded on its behalf by another state.[8]

Indeed, a state may cease to be independent without ceasing

---

[7] On the problem of equality of states, see E. D. Dickinson, *The Equality of States in International Law* (Cambridge, Mass., Harvard University Press, 1920) and H. Kelsen, "The Draft Declaration on Rights and Duties of States," *AJIL*, Vol. 44, No. 2 (April 1950), p. 259.

[8] See, e.g., *Case Concerning Rights of Nationals of the United States of America in Morocco*, [1952] I.C.J. Reports 176. Between 1871 and 1919, the states which composed the German Empire, a federation, retained a limited capacity to enter into diplomatic relations and treaties with foreign states. The temporary occupation and administration of a state by other states do not extinguish its statehood. Examples are the Dominican Republic from 1916 to 1924, when it was under United States military government, and Germany and Japan after World War II.

to be a state. This has happened, for example, when previously independent states became protectorates or members of certain federal unions. Conversely, territorial entities not previously regarded as states may suddenly or gradually acquire a measure of capacity to enter into treaties and other forms of official relations with other states without becoming independent.[9] "States may be said to fall into two general classifications, i.e. independent and dependent states."[10] Even entities possessed of little or no self-government are sometimes admitted to limited participation in the less political aspects of international affairs, such as postal relations.

The identity of a state and the continuity of its rights and duties in international law are not impaired by changes in its law, government, or constitutional structure, no matter how violent, at least so long as the core of its territory and population remain the same. This is a principle of great functional importance which facilitates transnational economic and other activities. In some states, violent revolutions occur almost every year. Private and governmental activities based on expectations of stability of the international legal order would be greatly hampered if all treaties and contracts binding the state lapsed every time a new government came into power. Even the absence of a recognized or effective central government for a number of years is not sufficient to destroy a state's identity. Similarly, a state cannot by changing its own law abrogate or modify its obligations under international law. But difficulties may arise in determining whether or not territorial losses or acquisitions have been so great as to result in the appearance of a new

---

[9] Examples are many. They include India between 1919 and 1947, when it was a party to numerous multilateral treaties, including the League of Nations Covenant and the United Nations Charter; the Byelorussian and Ukrainian Soviet Socialist Republics which are members of the United Nations and parties to many multilateral treaties; and Rhodesia (formerly Southern Rhodesia), which is a separate party to the General Agreement on Tariffs and Trade (GATT) and some other treaties. See, further, J. E. S. Fawcett, *The British Commonwealth in International Law* (London, Stevens & Sons, 1963).

[10] G. H. Hackworth, *Digest of International Law* (Washington, GPO, 1940-1944), Vol. I, p. 58.

state. Such difficulties are usually resolved by express or tacit agreement with other states.

When a state loses its identity through absorption into another state, its treaties for the most part come to an end. If, however, it retains some standing in international law despite the loss of independence, those of its treaties which are not incompatible with the new state of affairs continue in force. A new state does not automatically succeed to all the treaties of its predecessor and appears to have a large measure of freedom in choosing those by which it is to be bound. With respect to other obligations, including government contracts, the norms of state succession are not well settled. A state which absorbs another usually takes over its debts. Succession is often regulated by treaty. It is clear that a change of sovereignty, however accomplished, does not by itself extinguish or modify private property rights and personal relationships such as marriage. Similarly, it does not serve as an automatic repeal of the law previously in force in the territory concerned, with the possible exception of the constitution and some other branches of public law. The successor state is, of course, generally free to amend or replace pre-existing law by express enactment.

Recognition

Does a state exist in international law before it has been recognized by other states? Despite interminable controversy, no answer to this question seems to have won general acceptance. According to one theory, a state has no identity or standing in international law until it has been recognized by other states. Recognition has "constitutive" effect. According to another theory, a state exists and has rights and duties in international law as soon as it is effectively established and maintained as an entity with the essential attributes of statehood. Recognition merely "declares" this fact. Attempts to reconcile the two theories have been un-

11

successful. In practice, a new entity may be recognized as a state by some, but not all, other states for a considerable period of time. During this period, general international law operates to its full extent between the new state and those which have recognized it. With respect to the legal relations between the new entity and the non-recognizing states, the situation is far less clear. Practice exhibits a wide variety of attitudes; but in some situations a non-recognizing state has indicated, at least by implication, that the unrecognized entity has some if not all of the rights and duties of a state under general international law.

Recognition of a state should not be confused with recognition of its government. A state may continue to be recognized even though its government is not. The acts of an unrecognized government which is in effective control of a state may bind the state internationally.

Recognition may be accorded expressly or by implication. The test is actual intention. Acts which might imply recognition, such as the conclusion of an agreement with the entity in question, do not have this effect if the intent to recognize is expressly disavowed. For some purposes, recognition may have retroactive effect, but the recognizing state has a large measure of discretion in determining the extent of such effect.

A distinction is often drawn between recognition *de jure* (or full diplomatic recognition) and recognition *de facto*. The legal consequences of this distinction are far from clear. Recognition *de jure* frequently implies that the recognizing state has no reservations about the stability, effectiveness, or legitimacy of the recognized entity or government. Diplomatic relations are usually maintained only with governments recognized *de jure*. But even regimes tottering on the brink of extinction are sometimes accorded recognition *de jure* for political reasons. The term "recognition *de facto*" may conceal a variety of situations and attitudes. Expressly accorded "recognition *de facto*" appears to differ

little if at all from "recognition *de jure*" in legal consequences.[11]

A state is legally free to terminate or withdraw its recognition of another state or government, but the extent to
which such withdrawal may have retroactive effect is doubt-
ful. Breaking off diplomatic relations need not signify withdrawal of recognition. The United States, for example, continued to recognize *de jure* the Castro regime in Cuba after
breaking off diplomatic relations with it.

Territorial Sovereignty and Jurisdiction

Probably the most basic and ubiquitous function of international law is to prevent or minimize friction between
states by delimiting the sphere of their authority. Where
does the authority of one state end and that of another state
begin? In the absence of a commonly accepted answer to
this question, officials of two or more states might attempt
to exercise their powers at the same place and time. The
consequent confusion and conflicts not only would give rise
to friction and breaches of the peace between otherwise
friendly states, but would impose additional and probably
prohibitive risks on economic and other private activity. The
universally accepted principle that with some exceptions a
state has the exclusive right to exercise governmental authority within its territory and that consequently the officials of
one state may not exercise such authority within the territory of another state without the consent of the latter thus
serves to facilitate private activities as well as friendly relations between states.

Far less clear is the freedom of a state to attach legal consequences within its own territory to events which occur
outside its territory. It is universally recognized that a state

---

[11] Diplomatic relations need not be maintained even between governments
which recognize each other *de jure*. One possible legal difference between recognition *de jure* and recognition *de facto*, is that a government which has not
been recognized *de jure* may be unable to obtain control of property which its
state has in the territory of the other state.

13

may prescribe rules of conduct to be followed by its own nationals abroad—at least to the extent that such rules do not require violation of the laws of other states. The rules so prescribed may be enforced by sanctions imposed on the disobedient national by his state within its own territory. He may be punished when he returns or his property may be confiscated even if he does not return. But to what extent is a state free to punish foreigners for acts which they commit outside its territory? The answer would seem to depend on the balance of the interests involved. The interest of all states in the suppression of piracy on the high seas is so great that any state may punish this crime regardless of the nationality of the accused.[12] A state is also widely conceded the right to punish offenses against its security, credit, or the performance of its governmental functions, even when committed abroad by foreigners. There is controversy, however, over the right of a state to punish offenses against its nationals committed by foreigners abroad, and to extend the application of its laws designed to regulate commerce (such as anti-trust legislation) to transactions and activities outside its territory which affect its economic interests. In the absence of a treaty obligation, no state has a duty to extradite to another state persons whom the latter has convicted or accused of crimes.

Boundaries between adjacent states are commonly drawn by agreement. Where a navigable river serves as the boundary without further specification, the boundary runs along the middle of the main channel used for navigation (*thalweg*). In a non-navigable stream, the boundary runs along a line equidistant from the two banks. When a boundary river shifts itself to a new bed so rapidly that the change is immediately noticeable (avulsion), the boundary remains in the old bed, thus preventing sudden and unexpected changes in the relationships which may depend on the location of the boundary; but if the change is very gradual

---

12 For a definition of piracy, see Articles 15-17 of the Convention on the High Seas concluded in 1958 at Geneva.

14

(erosion and accretion), allowing time for readjustment of the interests affected, the boundary shifts with the river.

International rivers—i.e., rivers which form boundaries between states or flow through more than one state, and their tributaries—are subject to a large measure of control by the riparian states within their respective territories. It is increasingly recognized, however, that this control is not absolute, and that the interests of other states, particularly other riparians, must be taken into account. Upper riparian states are commonly accorded freedom of navigation to and from the sea. Navigation on many of the more important international rivers is regulated by treaties among the riparians and, in some cases, other interested states. In recent decades, the use of certain rivers for irrigation and power has come to overshadow in importance their use for navigation. There is a strong tendency to recognize that "each co-riparian state is entitled to a reasonable and equitable share in the beneficial uses of the waters of the drainage basin," but the modalities of such uses must commonly be determined by agreement.[13]

Acquisition of Territory

Modern international law began to develop in the era of "expansion of Europe"—the age of discovery, exploration, and acquisition of distant lands by the Europeans. Among the new needs which spurred the development of international law was that for norms to guide states in their efforts to establish and maintain title to many of these lands and to adjust conflicting claims. Jurists naturally turned to the Roman law of private property for guidance and brought over into international law the terms and concepts of occupation, cession, prescription, and accretion. Supplemented by the concept of conquest or subjugation, these became the traditionally accepted modes of acquisition of territory. Oc-

---

[13] See International Law Association, *Report of the Forty-Eighth Conference Held at New York, 1958*, pp. 99-102.

15

cupation is the method of establishing sovereignty over territory which previously belonged to no state (*terra nullius*). The requisite elements are manifestation of intention to acquire title and the exercise of effective control. The latter requirement has been at times satisfied, particularly in the case of small and uninhabited islands, by little more than symbolic acts of sovereignty. But claims based on such acts have caused many controversies.[14]

Cession is the mode of transfer of territorial sovereignty from one existing state to another by express agreement. Prescription is the method of acquiring title to territory (previously claimed by another state) through the exercise of effective and virtually uncontested control over a prolonged period of time, although international law contains no specification beyond "reasonableness" of the requisite length of the period. Accretion (or accession) is the addition of territory resulting from natural processes such as the deposit of alluvium (silt) on the shores or banks of a body of water. Conquest or subjugation is the acquisition of some or all of the territory of another state by force of arms. The conqueror must exercise effective control and manifest intention to establish his sovereignty. In practice, contests of arms have often led to transfers of territory by express agreement, i.e., cession, particularly when the defeated state remained in existence. Cession by peace treaty is not "conquest" in the traditional language of international law. In recent decades, the validity of territorial titles acquired as a result of use of force has been increasingly questioned, although a distinction is often drawn between lawful and unlawful (aggressive) uses of force. Territorial sovereignty, however established, may be lost not only through the transfer of title to another state, but also by abandonment. Abandoned territory reverts to the status of *terra nullius*. In practice, clear instances of abandonment have been rare.

---

[14] Controversy over territorial claims in Antarctica has been at least temporarily stilled by a treaty concluded in 1959 to which some fourteen states are parties. For text see *AJIL*, Vol. 54 (1960), No. 2 (April 1960), p. 476.

It requires not only cessation of exercise of control, but also manifestation of intention to relinquish title. "Relinquishment" by treaty is usually a form of transfer similar to cession and does not result in reversion to *terra nullius*.

The adequacy of the traditional concepts of the modes of acquisition and loss of territory is open to doubt. Not only do they fail to account for the sovereignty of a new state established either by revolution or by peaceful arrangement in a territory which previously belonged to another state, but they do not fully explain what has happened in a number of actual situations. Not infrequently, the real problem is which of two contestants has the stronger claim. In the solution of this problem, the emphasis is often placed not on the traditional distinctions between modes of acquisition or absolute compliance by either party with the traditionally stated requirement, but on other elements: a process of consolidation of title (which includes the length of time and relative strength of assertion and exercise of sovereignty, and recognition or acquiescence by other states), geographical contiguity or proximity, and perhaps the principle of self-determination.[15] The importance of effective control in the establishment and maintenance of territorial titles not only reflects the realities of power, but also serves the general interest in the exploitation of resources and in the facilitation of transnational economic activities, since in a land where no state really exercises control despite nominal claims of sovereignty the conditions requisite for the security of life, property, and contractual rights are not likely to exist.

The Law of the Sea

The sea has long been a highway for commerce and war as well as a provider of food and other resources. At times, particular states have made strong efforts to assert exclusive

15 R. Y. Jennings, *The Acquisition of Territory in International Law* (Manchester and New York, Manchester University Press and Oceana Publications, 1963).

control over vast maritime areas; but in modern international law it has come to be recognized that beyond a certain distance from the coast of a state the sea is free for reasonable use by all nations. This "freedom of the seas," which by and large serves the common interest of all or most states, includes freedom of navigation, freedom to fish and exploit other resources found above the bottom of the sea, freedom to lay cables and pipelines on the bottom of the sea, freedom to conduct military maneuvres and weapons tests, and in time of war freedom to attack the enemy and interrupt his communications. The general limitation on the exercise of these freedoms is that it must not unreasonably interfere with the use of the sea by other states.

The parts of the sea which are thus not subject to the sovereign control of any state are known as "the high seas." In time of peace, every state generally has exclusive control and jurisdiction on the high seas over the vessels which are entitled to fly its flag,[16] including the power to punish crimes committed on board such vessels, and must not interfere with the vessels of other states. There are, however, certain exceptions, of which the shared right to seize and punish pirates is the most consistently recognized. The freedom of the seas is further regulated by multilateral treaties on such matters as conservation of certain stocks of marine animals, safety at sea, pollution, protection of submarine cables, and slave trade.

The waters subject to the sovereignty of a state are of two kinds: internal (or inland) waters and the territorial sea (or territorial waters). Internal waters include not only rivers, lakes, and canals, but also maritime ports, harbors, certain bays, and, generally, all waters landward of the "base lines" from which the width of the territorial sea is measured. In internal waters, the sovereign rights and powers of the state are almost as great as on land. Foreign vessels have no

---

[16] Every state is generally free to grant the right to fly its flag to any vessel, but there should be some "genuine link" between the vessel and the state, and no vessel may have the right to fly the flags of two or more states.

general right of entry and navigation in internal waters, although merchant vessels of all friendly nations are commonly admitted to ports unless the latter are closed by express notice. While in port or other internal waters, foreign merchant vessels are subject to the jurisdiction of the coastal state, although the state of the flag of the vessel may also provide for the maintenance of order and for the punishment of crimes committed on board the vessel. By treaty and custom, important interoceanic canals are open to navigation by vessels of all states.

The territorial sea is a belt of water of specified width between the land territory (and internal waters) of a state on one side and the high seas on the other. It is most commonly measured from the low water line along the coast; but in certain circumstances, it may be measured from "straight baselines" which follow the general direction of the coast but are drawn between headlands, near-by islands, and other outlying points of land, thus enclosing considerable areas of internal waters, and from the outer limits of certain bays.

During the nineteenth century, the commonly accepted width of the territorial sea was three nautical miles. Some states attempted to claim more, but with the possible exception of Sweden and Norway were generally unsuccessful in enforcing such claims against the stronger maritime nations. (The four-mile claims of Sweden and Norway were widely respected.) Since World War I, the three-mile rule has encountered increasing opposition and today it cannot be said to command general support. At the 1958 and 1960 conferences on the law of the sea convoked by the United Nations, no agreement was reached on the width of the territorial sea.[17]

Within the territorial sea, the most important limitation on the coastal state's sovereignty is the right of innocent passage for vessels of other states. According to preponderant

17 See pp. 85-88.

19

opinion, this right extends to foreign warships, particularly in international straits, as well as to merchant vessels. Coastal states commonly abstain from exercising certain kinds of jurisdiction over foreign vessels in innocent passage. They may, however, temporarily suspend the right of innocent passage in specified areas of the territorial sea, except in international straits.[18]

Although the waters beyond the territorial sea are part of the high seas and not under the sovereignty of the coastal state, the latter may exercise reasonable control over foreign ships in "contiguous zones" adjacent to its territorial sea in order to prevent violations in its territory of its customs, fiscal, immigration, or sanitary regulations, and to maintain its security. In recent years, a growing number of states have established zones adjacent to their territorial sea in which they assert control over fishing. It has been widely recognized, furthermore, that a state may exercise exclusive jurisdiction and control, virtually amounting to sovereignty, over the natural resources of seabed adjacent to its territory and the subsoil beneath it to any depth at which the exploitation of such resources is feasible (the "continental shelf" doctrine). The coastal state may pursue and seize on the high seas a foreign vessel for violating its laws if the pursuit was begun within its territorial sea or contiguous zone and continued without interruption ("hot pursuit").[19]

---

[18] By treaty and general acquiescence, the Turkish Straits between the Black Sea and the Mediterranean are subject to a special regime, with certain limitations on the passage of warships.

[19] The very complex law of the sea has been presented here in barest outline. Much of it has been formulated in some detail in the four conventions concluded at Geneva in 1958. Not all states, however, have ratified these conventions, and some states have done so with reservations. One of the conventions, that on Fishing and Conservation of the Living Resources of the High Seas, had not come into force by the end of 1964 for lack of a sufficient number of ratifications. This convention, in the main, does not state already existing norms, but provides for a new system of regulation of fisheries. The extent to which some of the provisions of the other three conventions correspond to existing norms of general international law is uncertain. For texts, see U.S. Department of State *Bulletin*, Vol. 38, No. 992 (30 June 1958), p. 1110. For some recent trends, see pp. 85-89 below. For a comprehensive treatment of the law of the sea, see M. S. McDougal and W. T. Burke, *The Public Order of the Oceans* (New Haven and London, Yale University Press, 1962).

With the coming of powered flight in the twentieth century, the question of jurisdiction in airspace ceased to be academic and acquired great practical significance. Since World War I, it has been universally recognized that every state is sovereign in the airspace above its territory (including its territorial sea) and may exclude all foreign aircraft from it. In general international law, there is no right of innocent passage through such airspace. Only the airspace above the high seas is generally free, although some states have asserted and exercised without opposition the right to control for security and traffic purposes the flight of foreign aircraft above the high seas in certain zones adjacent to their airspace. The rigidity of national sovereignty in airspace has been mitigated by two widely accepted multilateral treaties —the Convention on International Civil Aviation and the Air Services Transit Agreement, both formulated at Chicago in 1944—and by numerous bilateral agreements which provide on a reciprocal basis for certain rights of entry and transit of aircraft and for the carriage of international air traffic. Aircraft, like ships, have the nationality of the state in which they are registered, and for certain purposes are subject to the jurisdiction of that state even when they are in foreign airspace. In contrast to aircraft, radio waves of foreign origin are commonly allowed to pass through the airspace of all states without special authorization so long as they cause no harm in subjacent states. The use of airspace for radio communication is largely regulated by the International Telecommunication Convention and ancillary agreements.

There is general consensus that sovereignty in airspace does not extend upward to infinity, and that space beyond

[20] United Nations General Assembly Res. 1962 (XVIII), 13 Dec. 1963. For a comprehensive treatment, see M. S. McDougal, H. D. Lasswell and I. A. Vlasic, *Law and Public Order in Space* (New Haven and London, Yale University Press, 1963).

a certain, as yet unspecified, altitude ("outer space") as well as the celestial bodies in it are not subject to national appropriation but are free for exploration and use by all states.[20]

Immunities from Jurisdiction

Sovereign states, their property, their agents, and their instrumentalities enjoy various immunities from the jurisdiction of other states, even in the territory of the latter. The head of a foreign state is personally inviolable and may not be prosecuted or sued in the courts. The extent to which the same sweeping immunities are possessed by the foreign states themselves and their property is a matter of controversy. According to the older "absolute" immunity doctrine, a foreign state is immune from suit without its consent regardless of the nature of the activity which has given rise to the suit against it; similarly, its property is immune from judicial attachment or execution. In recent decades, largely in response to the increase in state trading activities, a growing number of states and their courts have adopted the so-called "restrictive" doctrine of immunity, under which a foreign state may be sued on causes of action growing out of its commercial activities. Although the distinction between "commercial" and "sovereign" activities is not always clear, the application of the "restrictive" doctrine in numberless cases by the courts of many states indicates that international law does not require conformity to the "absolute" immunity doctrine. The "restrictive" doctrine serves the interests of the many states whose nationals do business with foreign governments or come in contact with their instrumentalities. It also tends to expand the rule of law. The property of a foreign state does not appear to be immune from expropriation or requisition with appropriate compensation if it is not used for diplomatic purposes.

Related to but distinct from "sovereign immunities" are

22

the immunities and privileges of diplomatic and consular establishments and their personnel. To facilitate diplomatic intercourse, foreign diplomatic missions of permanent character and the officers of diplomatic rank composing them are accorded sweeping immunities from the jurisdiction of the receiving state and are entitled to special protection by its authorities. Subject to minor exceptions, a foreign diplomat may not be arrested, prosecuted, sued, or taxed while he continues to be accredited to the receiving state, unless his government waives his immunity. With respect to his acts of a private character, however, he is not exempt from liability under the law of the receiving state, although in the absence of a waiver this liability may not be enforced prior to the termination of his diplomatic status (plus a reasonable time to leave the country). A former diplomat may be prosecuted or sued for his private acts if he chooses to remain in the receiving state. With respect to his official acts, however, immunity survives the termination of diplomatic status. Members of families of diplomatic officers generally share the immunities of the latter. The immunities of personnel below the rank of diplomatic officers are less well defined and may not extend to their private acts, especially if they are nationals of the receiving state. Foreign diplomats accredited to a third state enjoy certain immunities while in transit. The premises of a diplomatic mission are inviolable, as are its archives and correspondence, and are exempt from taxes. They must not be used, however, as places of asylum for fugitives from justice, or as prisons, since they remain part of the territory of the receiving state. Similar rules apply to the residences of foreign diplomatic officers.[21] The immunities of special (*ad hoc*) diplomatic missions are less well defined.

The immunities of foreign consular personnel are much more restricted than those of foreign diplomats. Under gen-

21 Diplomatic immunities are formulated in the Vienna Convention on Diplomatic Relations concluded in 1961. For text, see *AJIL*, Vol. 55, No. 4 (Oct. 1961), p. 1064.

eral international law, foreign consuls appear to be immune from local jurisdiction with respect to their official acts only. Their official archives and correspondence also enjoy immunity. Additional immunities, however, are generally provided in bilateral consular conventions.[22]

The immunities of members of foreign armed forces are largely defined in special agreements.[23] In the absence of such agreements, foreign military personnel appear to be immune from the jurisdiction of the receiving state only with respect to acts done in the performance of official duty, but they remain subject to the jurisdiction of their own state. Foreign warships in port or in the territorial sea are immune from the jurisdiction of the coastal state. Foreign military aircraft are also immune if their entry has been authorized by the territorial sovereign.

Intergovernmental organizations and their staffs possess certain immunities commonly defined by treaty. The extent of their immunities under general international law is controversial.

Nationality

Whether or not an individual is a national of a particular state is generally determined by the law of that state. Consequently, some individuals are stateless, that is, not entitled to claim the nationality of any state, while others have the nationality of two or more states (dual or plural nationality). Nationality is usually based on birth within the state (*jus soli*), descent from nationals of the state (*jus sanguinis*), marriage to a national of the state, or voluntary naturalization. A state is free to determine the extent to which it will employ any of these bases in granting or defining its

22 Consular immunities are formulated in the Vienna Convention on Consular Relations concluded in 1963. For text, see *AJIL,* Vol. 57, No. 4 (Oct. 1963), p. 995.

23 See, especially, the NATO Status of Forces Agreement, *United Nations Treaty Series,* Vol. 199, p. 67.

nationality. Marriage is no longer a basis of nationality in some states. In addition, the inhabitants of a territory transferred from one state to another normally acquire the nationality of the latter state, although they may be accorded an option. International law, however, imposes some limitations on the freedom of a state to claim individuals as its nationals. In particular, other states may be under no duty to recognize nationality not based on some genuine connection between the individual and the state claiming him.[24] There appear to be no limitations, however, on the freedom of a state to determine the conditions under which an individual loses its nationality (expatriation). The bond of nationality is regarded as one of "permanent allegiance" of the individual to the state, and entitles the state to exercise a wide measure of jurisdiction over him. It also entitles the state to protect him by diplomatic means against violations by other states of the standards of international law governing the treatment of aliens.

For many purposes, a corporation is regarded as having the nationality of the state under whose law it is organized. A state, however, may be entitled to protect the interests of its nationals in foreign corporations.

Treatment of Aliens and Responsibility of States

The need for some generally accepted standards to protect individuals and groups of individuals who have entered or are doing business in the territories of states other than their own has long been recognized, although their content has often been a matter of controversy. The absence of such standards would hamper if not make impossible many mutually beneficial transnational activities, such as trade, travel, and investment. Under general international law, a state is free to prevent the entry of a foreign national and to expel him even after an authorized entry. It is also free to control

---

[24] See the *Nottebohm Case*, [1955] I.C.J. Reports 4.

imports and exports and to impose tariff duties as it sees fit. It may deny to foreign nationals the right to own certain kinds of property (such as real property, ships, aircraft, or firearms), to organize corporations, to engage in business or other gainful occupations, and to participate in political activity. In these and many other matters, international law does not forbid a state to discriminate in favor of its own citizens, in the absence of treaty obligations to the contrary. Similarly, in many matters it may be free to discriminate between nationals of different foreign states. But in certain matters of fundamental importance to the individual—such as protection of life, personal liberty, and property—a state must generally treat foreign nationals at least as favorably as its own citizens. A large body of state practice and arbitral decisions indicates, moreover, that a state must live up to an international minimum standard of treatment of aliens, regardless of how it treats its own people. For example, if the officials of a state punish a foreign national without a fair trial, expose him to inhumane treatment in prison, or arbitrarily seize his property, the state cannot excuse itself by pointing out to similar treatment meted out to its own citizens. The more advanced nations of the West, moreover, have long insisted with a large measure of success that foreign private property may not be expropriated without full compensation. In recent decades, however, this norm and the very concept of an international minimum standard have been challenged by many less developed nations and the Soviet bloc.[25]

A violation of the standards of treatment of aliens exposes a state to diplomatic protests and claims of damages by the states whose nationals are the victims of the violation. Such protests and claims, however, are generally premature until the individuals concerned have exhausted all the remedies which may be available to them under the law of the state alleged to have committed the violation.

---

25 See pp. 75-85.

The principle of state responsibility, though often discussed in conjunction with the norms governing the treatment of aliens, extends far beyond the latter. A state is responsible for the acts and omissions of its government and its officials. Whenever such acts or omissions result in a violation of the rights of another state, appropriate reparation, such as payment of damages, is due.

The Law of Treaties

The vast majority of specific norms which regulate the relations of particular states is contained in treaties.[26] Quantitatively, therefore, treaties are the most important source of international law. But treaties are made within the framework of and in reliance upon norms which govern their conclusion, application, interpretation, revision, and termination. These norms are customary, since they are largely derived from the practice of states.

Treaties are agreements between states which are intended to be governed by international law.[27] As binding norms, they come into being when two or more states manifest consent to be bound by their terms. Such consent does not require any particular form. Even an oral manifestation of consent is binding, and in some situations consent may be implicit in the conduct of a state. Intention of the parties determines the dates on which a treaty comes into force and into operation. Some treaties do not become binding on a state until it has ratified, accepted, or approved them subsequently to their formulation or signature. This depends

---

[26] In addition to states, international organizations and certain other entities also have capacity to become parties to treaties. For convenience, only "states" are referred to in this survey of the law of treaties, but most of the latter is also applicable to international organizations and other entities possessed of the requisite capacity.

[27] The term "treaty" is used here in its broadest sense as embracing all such agreements, regardless of their form or the procedure by which they are concluded. It thus includes "treaties in simplified form" such as exchange-of-notes agreements, and even oral agreements. The U.N. International Law Commission has tentatively formulated the law of treaties in the form of draft articles. The successive parts of its draft appear in its 1962, 1963, and 1964 *Reports*.

on the intention of the states which have formulated the treaties, which may be manifested either in the treaties themselves or in other forms. A large and increasing number of treaties, however, become binding upon signature or upon the exchange of notes or other documents containing the terms of the agreements. A state may become a party (by accession or adherence) to a treaty formulated by other states only with the consent of the latter, but such consent may be given in the treaty itself.[28]

Every party to a treaty has a legal duty to perform it when it is in force and operation (*pacta sunt servanda*). Even if a treaty fails to conform to the constitutional requirements of a party, it is binding on the latter if it has been entered into on its behalf by the authority of a high official (such as the head of state, head of government, or foreign minister) who ordinarily represents the state in international relations. A treaty brought about by the use or threat of armed force in violation of international law is voidable at the option of the party which was the victim of the duress, or possibly even void *ab initio*. Undertakings which violate the rights of third states are widely believed to be invalid, but there is no clear-cut consensus to this effect.

Although a treaty ordinarily cannot impose obligations on non-consenting states, it is not impossible for two or more parties to confer rights on a state which is not a party to the treaty, if it accepts such rights expressly or by implication.

Ordinarily, a treaty should be interpreted in accordance with the manifested common design of the parties and so as to serve the major purposes sought to be accomplished by them. To this end, not only the text of the treaty, but all other relevant materials may be employed, including the records of the negotiations and subsequent conduct of the parties. Since treaties are normally made to record and

---

[28] On reservations to treaties see pp. 61 and 89.

secure certain shared expectations of the parties, it is important not to frustrate these expectations by formalistic or arbitrary interpretations. When a treaty has been commonly applied by the parties in a manner different from that contemplated at the time of its conclusion, such subsequent practice and the new expectations connected with it may properly form the basis of interpretation.

In principle, a treaty may be revised or terminated only with the express or implied consent of all the parties, but it is often provided in the treaty itself that any party may terminate it (or, in the case of a multilateral treaty, withdraw from it) by giving advance notice to that effect. An increasing number of multilateral treaties provide for revision by specified majorities of the parties. When a party does not expressly give its consent to the revision of a multilateral treaty, its failure to object to the revision often implies consent. These devices make for greater flexibility of the treaty network.

When a party breaches its duties under a treaty, other parties, if they are adversely affected by the breach, may denounce the treaty or suspend performance of their obligations under the provision which has been violated. War usually results in the suspension of many treaty relations between the parties and termination of some. If the performance of an obligation becomes impossible—as through the disappearance of the object—non-performance is excused. Very controversial is the effect on the continuing validity of a treaty of a change in the circumstances which existed at the time it was made. Although the existence in international law of a doctrine (sometimes called the doctrine of *rebus sic stantibus*) permitting unilateral abrogation of a treaty when certain circumstances have changed is widely admitted, there is lack of general agreement on the nature of such circumstances and of the requisite changes in them. The more liberal interpretations of the doctrine could make it a powerful instrument of peaceful change, but would threaten the stability of expectations based on treaties.[29]

The Use of Force

Before World War I, general international law did not restrict the freedom of states to resort to war as an instrument of policy, although it regulated the conduct of war. Paradoxically, it purported to limit resort to force "short of war," such as reprisals. In principle, reprisals were measures directed against a state which has violated international law and were designed to compel that state to conform to the law and to make adequate reparation for the injury caused by its unlawful conduct. Reprisals were justified only to the extent that they were not grossly out of proportion to the acts which provoked them. Armed force was often employed for the limited purpose of protecting the lives and property of a state's nationals in the territory of another state, but forcible intervention in the political affairs of an independent state was widely condemned by jurists as unlawful. In practice, these restrictions on the use of force were often disregarded.

Since World War I, the general revulsion against war has produced a series of treaties, declarations, and other manifestations of consensus that a state is no longer legally free to resort to war whenever its interests so require. No government today would openly claim the right to wage a war of aggression. In this sense, there exists a general consensus amounting to a legal norm that aggressive war is unlawful. In addition, it is widely believed that the United Nations Charter permits a state to use force against another state in only two situations: (1) in individual or collective self-defense; or (2) pursuant to the decision of a competent international organ. Neither "aggression" nor "self-defense,"

---

[29] On some effects of changes of sovereignty on treaties, see pp. 10-11. When territory is transferred by cession, most of the treaties of the previous sovereign cease to apply.

however, have been authoritatively defined (and perhaps cannot be), and there is much controversy over the precise scope and meaning of the new norms restricting the use of force. It is generally agreed that these restrictions apply to all inter-state uses of force, whether they are called "war" or "force short of war." Forcible reprisals are apparently no longer lawful.[30] Although these new norms have undoubtedly had a restraining effect on some states, it would be an exaggeration to say that they have been highly effective.

The conduct of war is regulated by many norms of varying degrees of specificity and effectiveness which have been largely incorporated in multilateral treaties. There is little effective regulation of the choice of weapons, although the prohibition against the use of poison gas has been widely respected after World War I, but detailed rules govern the treatment of prisoners of war and of the inhabitants of occupied enemy territory, as well as the behavior of belligerents toward neutral states and vice versa. Many of the norms of war and neutrality have been applied in some civil wars. Technological and political changes, however, have rendered obsolete much of the traditional law of neutral rights at sea. Similarly, the coming of the airplane and the missile has obliterated many of the traditional distinctions between the armed forces and the civilians as objects of attack. The prohibition of aggressive war and the provisions of the United Nations Charter are widely believed to permit a non-belligerent to discriminate against the aggressor and in favor of the victim of aggression, thus doing away with the traditional neutral duty of impartiality.

The Application and Sanctions of International Law

It has been well pointed out that "the daily reliance upon international law in the normal relations between states far exceeds in frequency, and probably in importance, its

---

[30] Cf. *The Corfu Channel Case*, [1949] I. C. J. Reports 4, 34-35.

role as a basis for settlement of differences."[31] International law forms the framework within which all transnational activity, public and private, takes place. Minor breaches of the law occur frequently, but only exceptionally do states deliberately break through the framework to commit gross and persistent violations. This usually happens only in a major crisis when the very existence of a nation seems to be at stake. Even when a nation deliberately violates the law, it seeks to justify its conduct by reinterpreting the relevant norms or misrepresenting the facts.

The reasons why the law is obeyed in any system of public order may be summarized under three headings: (1) self-interest; (2) sense of moral obligation; and (3) habit. Of the three, self-interest is probably the most basic reason why international law is observed. Its norms have been developed by states to serve common interests and to facilitate mutual relations. Consequently, so long as states continue to be guided by these purposes, they are not likely to disregard the relevant norms. Probably the most important sanction of international law is the fear of disruption of desired relationships regulated by it and of retaliation. If a state, for example, persistently disregards diplomatic immunities, it may be exposed to retaliation in the form of denial of similar immunities to its representatives abroad, or, in a particularly flagrant case, it may find other states unwilling to maintain diplomatic relations with it. Similarly, a state which persistently violates the freedom of the seas invites retaliation and impairment of its maritime trade with the rest of the world. The sense of moral obligation should not be minimized as a reason for law observance, but its force varies from nation to nation and from individual to individual. At times, moreover, moral principle may clash with a legal

---

31 W. W. Bishop, Jr., *International Law: Cases and Materials* (Boston and Toronto, Little, Brown and Company, 2nd ed., 1962), p. 57.

32 Cf. R. A. Falk, "The Adequacy of Contemporary Theories of International Law—Gaps in Legal Thinking," *Virginia Law Review*, Vol. 50, No. 2 (March 1964), pp. 258-260.

norm. Habit is an important factor in the routine observance of the law when the vital interests of a nation are not at stake.[32]

International law does serve as a set of standards to which appeal is made when disputes arise between states. It may be invoked in negotiations between the parties to the dispute or provide the basis for the decision of an international tribunal. Reference of disputes to international tribunals, however, is still rare. In principle, the power of the International Court of Justice to decide a dispute between two states rests on the consent of both parties, although such consent may be given in general terms before the dispute has arisen by acceptance of the compulsory jurisdiction of the Court under the so-called "optional clause" in Article 36 of the Court's Statute or by a provision in another treaty. Similarly, resort to arbitration depends on the consent of the parties. The International Court, however, may also give "advisory opinions" on legal questions at the request of certain organs of the United Nations and some other international organizations.

International law is also often applied by national courts when it is relevant to a controversy between private persons or between a private person and a government. In some nations, constitutions or statutes expressly direct the courts to apply international law; in others, a similar result has been brought about by judicial decision.[33]

The "Sources" of International Law

How does an international court or a national decision-maker find out what the norms of international law are? Article 38 of the Statute of the International Court of Justice provides in part:

---

[33] See, e.g., L. Erades and W. L. Gould, *The Relation Between International Law and Municipal Law in the Netherlands and in the United States: A Comparative Study* (Leyden and New York, A. W. Sythoff and Oceana Publications, 1961). On the International Court, see S. Rosenne, *The Law and Practice of the International Court* (Leyden, A. W. Sythoff, 1965).

1. The Court, whose function is to decide in accordance with international law such disputes as are submitted to it, shall apply:
   a. international conventions, whether general or particular, establishing rules expressly recognized by the contesting state;
   b. international custom, as evidence of a general practice accepted as law;
   c. the general principles of law recognized by civilized nations;
   d. subject to the provisions of Article 59, judicial decisions and the teachings of the most highly qualified publicists of the various nations, as subsidiary means for the determination of rules of law. . . .

Section 1 (a) of this article means that states are bound by the norms of valid and existing treaties which they have expressly accepted. It is an expression of the principle *pacta sunt servanda* and is relatively easy to apply. The norms contained in treaties constitute "conventional international law" and are usually a form of "particular" rather than "general" international law. A state, of course, is generally not bound by a treaty to which it is not a party. But a treaty may also record the parties' understanding of a norm of general international law and thus serve as evidence of the latter.

Much less definite is the meaning of section 1 (b) of Article 38. It is generally understood to refer to "customary international law." But how is the existence of a "custom" established? And what is "general practice"? According to the traditional view, customary international law is created by uniformities in the actual conduct of many states if such conduct is motivated or accompanied by a conviction that it is required or permitted by international law (*opinio juris sive necessitatis*). The artificiality of this construction and the difficulties it may cause—particularly in an era of rapid change—are patent. How many states must engage in the requisite practice before it becomes "general"? How is the existence of *opinio juris* to be ascertained? Are words, as distinguished from acts, of any significance? There is no doubt that many norms of international law have originated

34

in what Myres S. McDougal of Yale University likes to call "the process of reciprocal claims and mutual tolerances" of states over a number of years. But in an era of rapid change how can the law grow if the requirement of "general practice" accompanied by *opinio juris* is rigidly applied? How can there be a conviction that international law already requires or permits a certain kind of conduct if there has been no previous practice in the matter? The importance of this problem may be illustrated by the nascent law of outer space. Is there today a norm forbidding states to claim sovereignty over celestial bodies such as the Moon? As already noted, the General Assembly unanimously proclaimed in 1963 the principle that "celestial bodies are not subject to national appropriation"; as yet, however, there has been no occasion for any state to take specific action with respect to this matter. Is the verbal expression of general consensus in the General Assembly resolution of no value as indicating what the law is and how any future claims to the Moon are to be treated?

Indeed, it may be asked why "custom" or "general practice" should be binding on states. The answer must be sought not in legal abstractions but in the realities of international life. Uniformity of conduct and the process of "reciprocal claims and mutual tolerances" often create expectations of continuation of the same kind of conduct. States and other interested entities, including private persons, develop their policies and plan their actions on the basis of such expectations. There is, therefore, a common interest in the fulfillment of these expectations and in the stability of conduct. This interest is translated into the doctrine that "custom" or "general practice" creates legally binding norms. But expectations may rest not only on actual conduct, but also on other forms of communication, including the verbal. This is quite clear in the case of treaties. Statements or declarations not binding as treaties may also give rise to reasonable expectations. If such statements or declarations emanate

35

from a large number of states and purport to deal with a legal matter, they may be regarded in some circumstances as indications of a general consensus amounting to a norm of general international law. Even unperfected treaty drafts are occasionally cited as evidence of consensus. It is misleading, therefore, to regard "custom" or "general practice", if these terms are interpreted narrowly, as the ultimate basis of general international law. The latter must be found in the general consensus and expectations of states, of which "custom" or "general practice" is but one form of evidence.[34] If section 1 (b) of Article 38 of the Court's Statute is not to be misleading, it should be read somewhat as follows: "The practice of states as evidence of a general consensus or expectations accepted as law."

The recognition that general international law rests on the consensus of states does not, of course, suffice to dispose of all difficulties. How can a change in the consensus be brought about or ascertained and applied without violating existing law? And does the dissent of one state or a small group of states suffice to prevent a norm from being one of *general* international law? In reality, the practice which indicates the existence of a consensus may not be universal. It may be restricted to a certain number of states simply because other states have not had the occasion to act in the matter or express any view of it. Their silence, however, may be interpreted as acquiescence rather than dissent. More difficult is a situation in which some states expressly reject, by acts or words, a norm accepted by other states. Is such rejection decisive? Does a norm cease to exist as one of general international law when, after a period of general acceptance, it is challenged by some states while others insist on its continued and universal validity? And what is the significance of discrepancies between words and deeds? A state may verbally reject a norm while actually conforming to it;

---

[34] This conclusion is supported by a careful study of the decisions and opinions of national and international decision-makers which is too long to be presented here.

36

conversely, its acts may be at variance with a norm which it purports to accept. Are deeds always more important than words?

No general answers to these perplexing and crucial questions will be attempted here, if indeed such answers are possible. These questions are presented here to show the inadequacy of existing doctrines of "sources" of general international law and to stress the uncertainty and fluidity of much of "custom." Authoritative decision-makers may answer these questions expressly or by implication with reference to the specific situations which face them and in the light of all the factors which they deem relevant, often including their conceptions of the purposes to be served by their decisions. The uncertainty of much of customary international law has led to a movement for its "codification," that is, express formulation, mainly in the form of multilateral treaties. A number of such treaties are already in force. Though not ratified by some states, such treaties are often used as evidence of general international law. But other efforts at codification have been less successful and have increased rather than diminished the uncertainties of general international law.

Decision-makers in passing on questions of international law sometimes resort to analogies from other (municipal) legal systems and to general principles which appear to be essential to the just and orderly operation of any legal system. This is recognized and sanctioned by section 1 (c) of Article 38 of the Statute. Controversy over the precise meaning of "general principles of law" and the methods of ascertaining them continues. But the permissibility of resort to them contributes to the flexibility of international law and gives the decision-makers another tool with which to promote its growth.

Section 1 (d) appears to stress the "subsidiary" role of judicial decisions and opinions of writers as means of ascertaining the law. This is somewhat misleading. Despite the

37

language of Article 59 of the Statute,[35] the International Court of Justice does not hesitate to attach great weight to its own previous decisions. Arbitral awards and the decisions of national courts are often relied upon by other decision-makers, although references to them in the Court's opinions are scarce.

Read literally, the language of Article 38 of the Court's Statute is hardly a trustworthy guide to the "sources" of international law. Paradoxically, this very inadequacy, by leaving much room for interpretation and supplementation, may tend to promote the process of change in international law rather than hold it within the strict confines of the conceptions prevalent when the Statute of the Permanent Court of International Justice, from which it was largely copied, was drafted (i.e., in 1920).

What Is International Law?

Is the definition of international law given by Oppenheim[36] still adequate? The answer must be no. Indeed, every important element in it can now be challenged.

First, it is now generally recognized that not only "states," but also public international organizations have rights and duties under international law, even though they may not have *all* of the rights and duties that states have.[37] More controversial but no longer untenable is the view that even individuals and other private persons may have some such rights and duties.[38] It is no longer possible, therefore, to regard international law as governing relations solely be-

---

[35] "The decision of the Court has no binding force except between the parties and in respect of that particular case."

[36] See p. 8.

[37] See, e.g., *Reparation for Injuries Suffered in the Service of the United Nations,* Advisory Opinion, [1949] I. C. J. Reports 174; D. W. Bowett, *The Law of International Institutions* (London, Stevens & Sons, 1963), pp. 273-310. The Holy See has long been regarded as having rights and duties under international law.

[38] For a balanced account, see W. Friedmann, *The Changing Structure of International Law* (New York, Columbia University Press, 1964), pp. 221-249.

tween states. It may also govern relations between states and international organizations, between two or more international organizations, between states and private persons, and between international organizations and private persons.[39] Consequently, international law can no longer be defined in terms of the entities whose relations it governs. The distinctive feature of international law must be sought elsewhere. This feature appears in the authority by which international law is made. International law, unlike municipal law, is created not by a single state, but by two or more states jointly.[40] Even this may prove, however, to be an inadequate conception as international organs created by states acquire more and more influence of their own.

Second, it is now widely recognized that international law consists not only of "customary and conventional rules," but also of "general principles of law."

Third, the very conception that international law is a "body of rules" now stands challenged as static and inadequate. "It is a commonplace that law is a process, not a body of self-executing rules . . ."[41] Like all living law, international law does not stand still but is continuously reinterpreted and reshaped in the very process of its application by authoritative decision-makers, national and international. Norms play an important role in this process, but no living norm retains the same content for long. Since no two fact situations are exactly alike, decision-makers continually face the task of deciding whether to apply a norm to a new situation. This task often cannot be performed by a mechanical application of legal logic, but requires the making of a value judgment as to the purposes which would or would not be served by the application of the norm. The need for making

39 See, e.g., *Effect of Awards of Compensation Made by the United Nations Administrative Tribunal*, Advisory Opinion, [1954] I. C. J. Reports 4.

40 H. Kelsen, *Principles of International Law* (New York, Rinehart & Co., 1952) , p. 201.

41 M. A. Kaplan and N. deB. Katzenback, *The Political Foundations of International Law* (New York and London, John Wiley & Sons, 1961) , p. 231 (and cf. pp. 19-29) ; and see, generally, the writings of Myres S. McDougal.

such judgments is faced by even the most "impartial" judges. The direction in which the law is developing at any given time is thus inescapably influenced by the decision-makers' conceptions of what that direction should be. "What the law is" (*lex lata*) can never be entirely separated from "what the law ought to be" (*lex ferenda*).[42]

The task of deciding whether to apply a norm to a new situation is performed not only by international decision-makers such as the judges of international courts, but also, and more frequently, by national governments as they appraise each other's actions and responses in the international arena. In this "process of reciprocal claims and mutual tolerances," they are guided not only by their conceptions of the general interest of the world community, but also, and mainly, by the particular interests of their nations. Much of international law thus rests not on abstract formulations of "the general interest," but on the congruence or reasonable accommodation of the interests of many nations producing a consensus which can be translated into legal terms.

The conception of international law as a process of change and development through decisions into which value judgments enter does not exclude recognition of the existence of many norms of a high degree of specificity and stability. Most norms have an identifiable "hard core" in the sense that most decision-makers would agree that they are applicable in certain situations.[43] But a static conception of international law as a mere "body of rules" derived from technically defined "sources," though useful for certain purposes, is not helpful in the task of meeting the new challenges and demands addressed to international law in a divided and dynamic world.

---

[42] See, e.g., C. W. Jenks, *The Prospects of International Adjudication* (London and Dobbs Ferry, Stevens & Sons and Oceana Publications, 1964), pp. 617-662, and the writings of McDougal.

[43] Cf. R. A. Falk, *op. cit.*, pp. 240-242.

The great fratricidal war of the West, commonly known as World War I, paved the way for the seizure of power in Russia by the Bolshevik (later Communist) Party which, under the leadership of Lenin, was dedicated to the overthrow of the existing world order. The future organization of mankind was envisioned as a classless society in which neither the state nor law would be needed and in which no coercive institutions would interfere with the full flowering of human dignity. In the new world commonwealth, there would be no place for international law. The history of the world was seen by the Communists as one of struggle between antagonistic classes in which there could be no lasting compromise, and which would end with the triumph of the proletariat over its oppressors—the capitalists.

At the very time the cataclysmic transformation of government and society was taking place in Russia, new demands were being addressed to international law. The increasing costs of modern warfare and the holocaust of World War I made men turn hopefully to international law as possible protection against global slaughter. The success or failure of international law came increasingly to be judged in terms of prevention of war. Treaties against war, such as the 1928 Peace Pact of Paris and numerous non-aggression pacts, were concluded. The League of Nations represented an attempt to establish a collective security system. Efforts were made to achieve disarmament by general agreement. There was a movement to have states submit their disputes to international tribunals for settlement, and a Permanent Court of International Justice was set up within the framework of the League system.

The failure of international law to preserve peace and the flagrant violation by the Axis powers of their treaty obligations were the primary causes of the feeling, by the end of the inter-war period, that a crisis had developed in international

41

law. The arrogant repudiation by totalitarian ideologies—both Fascist and Communist—of many of the values and institutions previously shared by all Western nations, and the dynamic aggressiveness with which totalitarian elites sought to satisfy obsessive desires for national self-assertion and aggrandizement deepened the sense of crisis.

New demands of another type addressed to international law had become faintly visible after World War I. Non-Western peoples were groping for legal justification of their desires for the revision or abrogation of "unequal" treaties (particularly those by which the Western powers had obtained extraterritorial jurisdiction and other special privileges), for an end to racial discrimination, and, in many cases, for independence. In these demands, the non-Western peoples were encouraged by the liberal traditions of the West as well as by the ardent Bolshevik espousal of slogans of sovereignty, equality, self-determination, "anti-imperialism," and the invalidity of "unequal" treaties.

In the attempts to get rid of "unequal" treaties, some non-Western nations appealed to the controversial doctrine of *rebus sic stantibus*—the doctrine that unilateral denunciation of a treaty may be justified by certain changes in circumstances.[44] Attempts at unilateral termination of Western privileges were generally unsuccessful, but the Western powers began gradually to give up their extraterritorial jurisdiction and almost all vestiges of this institution have now disappeared. The process was orderly and put no great strain on international law. It was political in nature and gave rise to no new generally accepted norms of international law.

In 1919, in an effort to limit racial discriminatory practices in the West, Japan, the strongest Asian nation, attempted to have inserted in the League of Nations Covenant a provision whereby the parties would agree to accord "as soon as pos-

---

[44] See *Law of Treaties: Draft Convention, with Comment*, Harvard Research in International Law, in *AJIL*, Vol. 29, No. 4 (Oct. 1935), Special Supplement, pp. 1115-1118. At that time there was little or no attempt to declare such treaties void *ab initio*. Cf., p. 93.

sible," equal treatment to all alien nationals of League members "making no distinction, either in law or in fact, on account of their race or nationality." [45] This proposal, which would have required the United States (if it had become a League member) and other Western powers to repeal discriminatory provisions in, for example, their immigration and alien landholding laws, failed of adoption. Shortly thereafter the United States Congress forbade all Japanese immigration. Japan protested bitterly against this further manifestation of racial discrimination but found nothing in international law to support its protest, which was rejected by the United States. [46]

The idea that all peoples are entitled to self-determination had its origins in the liberal thought of the Enlightenment and the American and French Revolutions. But it was not until World War I that the idea came to be widely echoed in the official pronouncements of governments and statesmen. Within a few days of its establishment, the Soviet government proclaimed "the right of the peoples of Russia to free self-determination up to and including separation and the formation of an independent state." [47] The right of self-determination was explicitly or implicitly recognized in the statements of war aims issued by Prime Minister Lloyd George and President Wilson. In part, these were meant to counter the attractiveness of Bolshevik slogans. [48] But the Western states stopped short of advocating self-determina-

[45] D. Hunter Miller, *The Drafting of the Covenant* (New York, Putnam, 1928), Vol. 1, p. 183.

[46] After World II, many discriminatory provisions in United States law were eliminated.

[47] Ministerstvo Inostrannykh Del SSSR, *Dokumenty Vneshnei Politiki SSSR* (Moscow, Gosudarstvennoie Izdatel'stvo Politicheskoi Literatury, 1957—), Vol. 1, pp. 14-15. Self-determination was also implied in the Soviet "Decree on Peace" of 8 November 1917, which purported to lay down the principles of a just peace. *Ibid.*, pp. 11-14, 69. Unless otherwise specified, all translations are those of the author.

[48] See A. J. Mayer, *Wilson vs. Lenin: Political Origins of the New Diplomacy 1917-1918* (Cleveland and New York, The World Publishing Co., 1964). For a recent Soviet study, see G. Starushenko, *The Principle of National Self-Determination in Soviet Foreign Policy* (Moscow, Foreign Languages Publishing House, n.d.).

tion for their own colonies or other territorial possessions; it was merely to be an element in the disposition of those enemy territories whose fate was to be decided in the peace settlement.

The principle of self-determination was but imperfectly reflected in the peace treaties that concluded World War I. The territorial settlements embodied in these treaties were the result of compromises in which numerous factors were taken into account. One such compromise was the system of mandates under which the former German colonies and the Middle Eastern territories detached from Turkey were placed. Only in the case of the latter did Article 22 of the League Covenant mention eventual independence as a goal. No such promise was made to the peoples of the mandated territories in Africa and Oceania.

During the inter-war period, self-determination was generally regarded in the West as a policy to be applied selectively when circumstances required, rather than as a legal right of all peoples. The ideal of government with the consent of the governed continued to live, however, and contributed to the beginning of the process of decolonization. Great Britain relaxed its hold over Egypt and Iraq and introduced a greater measure of self-government in some of its colonies. The British dominions became virtually independent. The United States promised independence to the Philippines after a ten-year transitional period. In India, pressure for emancipation from British rule increased. In the meantime, the Soviet government continued to emphasize the right of self-determination in a number of its treaties with neighboring states.[49] The Soviet Constitution purported to give each of the constituent republic of the Soviet Union the right of secession.

It was not until after World War II, when pressure from the increasingly nationalistic educated elites of the non-West-

[49] See, for example, T. A. Taracouzio, *The Soviet Union and International Law* (New York, Macmillan, 1935), pp. 31-32, 253, 256, 279.

ern peoples became more effective, that self-determination as a right of all colonial peoples came to be more generally accepted. The drive for emancipation was given further support by Articles 1 (2) and 55 of the United Nations Charter which mentioned "respect for the principle of equal rights and self-determination of peoples" as a basis for "friendly relations among nations." Subsequent United Nations resolutions, while they do not have the force of treaties, went even further. By 1960, no nation felt able to oppose a declaration that self-determination and independence are inalienable rights of all peoples.[50]

---

[50] See General Assembly Res. 1514 (XV), 14 Dec. 1960.

THE SOVIET UNION AND INTERNATIONAL LAW

NOTHING IN THE BACKGROUND of the Communist leaders who seized power in Russia in 1917 predisposed them favorably toward international law. Like all law, it was to be regarded by Marxists as an instrument of the policy of the ruling class—namely, the "capitalist" class, under whose rule it had been developed. But the young Soviet republic, surrounded by "capitalist" states it was too weak to defy openly, needed peace and trade. Unhesitatingly, the Soviet leaders turned to international law as a means of protection and of necessary cooperation with the outside world. They were prompt to invoke international law against the hostile activities of Western powers. As early as 1921, "international law" was expressly laid down in a German-Soviet bilateral agreement as a standard to be applied in certain matters by these countries in their relations with each other.[51]

In 1946, the Central Committee of the All-Union Communist Party directed that special attention be given to the study of international law.[52] A steadily swelling stream of books, articles, and other publications on international law has since been pouring off the Soviet presses. This stream has become noticeably larger since the end of late-Stalin isolationism. From the time of the Twentieth Congress of the Communist Party in 1956, at which the "cult of personality" was first denounced, until early 1962, more works on international law are said to have appeared in the Soviet Union than in the forty previous years of the existence of the Soviet state.[53] In 1957, a Soviet Association of Inter-

51 Ministerstvo Inostrannykh Del SSSR, *Dokumenty Vneshnei Politiki SSSR, op. cit.*, Vol. 3 (1959) , p. 99, Arts. 8, 10, 13.

52 *Kul'tura i Zhizn*, 20 Nov. 1946.

53 G. I. Tunkin, "XXII S'ezd KPSS i Zadachi Sovetskoi Nauki Mezhdunarodnogo Prava," *Sovetskoie Gosudarstvo i Pravo*, No. 5 (1962) , p. 4.

national Law was formed. It publishes a Soviet yearbook of international law, in which the principal articles are accompanied by summaries in English. This Association has joined the world-wide International Law Association. The textbook of international law published by the Soviet Academy of Sciences in 1957 has been translated and widely distributed in several languages, including English.[54] Many Western works on international law have been translated and published in the Soviet Union. Soviet representatives take an active and influential part in international conferences for the codification and development of international law (such as the 1958 and 1960 United Nations Conferences on the Law of the Sea held at Geneva and the 1961 United Nations Conference on Diplomatic Intercourse and Immunities at Vienna) and in the work of the Sixth Committee of the United Nations General Assembly. Soviet spokesmen in and out of the United Nations often invoke international law in support of their contentions and call for its strict observance.

A Pragmatic Approach

The basic Soviet attitude toward international law was developed fairly rapidly under the combined pressure of practical need and Marxist doctrine. The problem of reconciling the apparent acceptance of an international law binding on Communist and non-Communist governments alike with the Marxist conception of law has been a perennial source of difficulty for Marxist legal theoreticians; but it has not been allowed to stand in the way of the pragmatic use of international law in the interests of Soviet policy. This pragmatic approach has remained substantially the same to this day, despite frequent variations in formulation and sometimes acrimonious discussion of the finer points

---

[54] Academy of Sciences of the USSR, Institute of State and Law, *International Law* (Moscow, Foreign Languages Publishing House, [1961]).

[55] See R. A. Ramundo, *The (Soviet) Socialist Theory of International Law* (Washington, George Washington University, Institute for Sino-Soviet Studies, Series No. 1, Jan. 1964).

by Soviet jurists.[55] All doctrines, formulations, and applications of international law are appraised in terms of their usefulness to the Communist cause.

The idea that during the "time of transition" from capitalism to the classless society there is room for the application of certain legal norms between the states of the two camps was formulated by the first outstanding Soviet theoretician in the field, E. A. Korovin, as early as 1924 in *International Law of the Time of Transition*. In 1935, E. B. Pashukanis pointed out that the Soviet Union could use to its advantage the existing formal structure of international law.[56] In the late Stalin era, F. I. Kozhevnikov baldly stated the Soviet attitude in these words:

> Those institutions in international law which can facilitate the execution of the stated tasks of the USSR are recognized and applied by the USSR, and those institutions which conflict in any manner with these purposes are rejected by the USSR.[57]

A clue to the Soviet approach, at least before 1964, is the reference to "struggle" and "cooperation" in many Soviet definitions of international law. The idea that international law can be useful in struggles between states is a valid insight, for, in the past, states have often employed it to advance their own interests as against the interests of other states.[58] But the *order* in which the words "struggle" and "cooperation" appear in Soviet definitions of international law, as well as the Communist philosophy of history, symbolize the relative importance of the two in Soviet eyes.

[56] E. A. Korovin, *Mezhdunarodnoie Pravo Perekhodnogo Vremeni* (2nd ed., Moscow, Gosizdat, 1924), and E. B. Pashukanis, *Ocherki po Mezhdunarodnomu Pravu* (Moscow, Sovetskoie Zakonodatel'stvo, 1935).

[57] *Sovetskoie Gosudarstvo i Mezhdunarodnoie Pravo* (Moscow, Yuridicheskoie Izdatel'stvo, 1948), p. 25, as translated in J. N. Hazard, *Law and Social Change in the USSR* (Toronto, Carswell, 1953), p. 275. Further, he explained that the various important principles of international law accepted by the Soviet Union, including those of the binding force of treaties, inviolability of a state's territory, "sovereign equality," and non-intervention, should be interpreted flexibly rather than in an "abstractly dogmatic" manner. *Ibid.*, pp. 103-104, 134, 182-183, 255-256.

[58] Many Western political scientists regard conflict as the essence of world politics.

A key Soviet definition of international law was that of A. Y. Vishinsky, who, in 1948, called it "the sum total of the norms regulating relations between states in the process of their struggle and cooperation, expressing the will of the ruling classes of these states and secured by coercion exercised by states individually or collectively."[59] The change in style of Soviet domestic and foreign policy that followed the death of Stalin was reflected in the tone, but not in the substance, of the utterances of leading Soviet jurists. Vishinsky's definition survived Stalin and himself. In the textbook of international law published in 1957 by the Institute of State and Law of the Soviet Academy of Sciences, the only significant change in the definition is the addition of a reference to "peaceful coexistence," which reflects a new emphasis in Soviet foreign policy after the death of Stalin.[60] Further modification of the definition has been suggested by G. I. Tunkin who, as head of the Treaty and Legal Department of the Soviet Ministry for Foreign Affairs, is the official international law adviser of the Soviet government. Tunkin has suggested the addition of the idea that international legal norms are created by agreement among states; de-emphasis of the role of coercion in securing the observance of international law; and finally, reflection of the decision of the Twenty-second Congress of the Communist Party that the Soviet state is no longer ruled by a class but by the whole people. But Tunkin also affirms that the principles and norms of general international law "reflect the struggle and cooperation of states, and, first of all, of states of the two systems."[61]

The textbook of international law published in 1964 by the Soviet Institute of International Relations drops the reference to "struggle and cooperation" in its definition of international law, which reads as follows:

59 A. Y. Vishinsky, "Mezhdunarodnoie Pravo i Mezhdunarodnaia Organizatsiia," *Sovetskoie Gosudarstvo i Pravo*, No. 1 (1948), p. 22 .The elements of this definition are traceable back to 1938. See Raimundo, *op. cit.*, p. 4.
60 Academy of Sciences of the USSR . . . , *International Law*, *op. cit.*, p. 7.
61 Tunkin, "XXII S'ezd KPSS . . . ," *op. cit.*, pp. 3, 12-13.

Contemporary international law has as its principal content the generally recognized principles and norms designed to regulate the most varied relations of sovereign wills between the subjects of international community on the basis and for the purpose of effectively securing international peace, and above all peaceful coexistence in some cases and socialist internationalism in others.

The degree and forms of such securing are determined by the very character of the given international legal order. Under the conditions of peaceful coexistence, the element of coercion is greatly limited, but not excluded. In the world system of socialism all legal principles and norms, being based on socialist internationalism and therefore having a fundamentally different content, are invariably observed, and their securing is subordinated to this content.[62]

The change appears to stem primarily from the increased stress on the role of international law in the relations between the socialist states and between the latter and the new nations. It is reaffirmed that the contemporary era is one of struggle between the socialist and the capitalist systems.[63]

It is the Soviet stress on antagonism rather than cooperation as the primary characteristic of the relations between the states of "the two systems" that sets narrow limits to the role of international law in world affairs. Some principles of international law of great generality and, hence, of uncertain content, have served Soviet leaders as slogans in their ideological struggle against the capitalist states. Among the more traditional of these principles are sovereignty, territorial inviolability and equality of states, and non-intervention. Other principles invoked, such as non-aggression and self-determination, for which Soviet spokesmen claim a major share of credit, are of more recent origin and are more controversial. All these principles, both old and new, have been used by the Soviet leaders both defensively and offensively.

Defensively, these principles have been employed to deter or stigmatize actions detrimental to the Soviet Union by

---

[62] F. I. Kozhevnikov, ed., *Mezhdunarodnoie Pravo* (Moscow, Izdatel'stvo Instituta "Mezhdunarodnye Otnosheniia," 1964), p. 32.

[63] *Ibid.*, pp. 30, 68-80.

other states. When the Soviet republic was weak, they were useful in mobilizing outside public opinion against real or feared intervention by the "capitalist" states in Soviet affairs, and, subsequently, against aggression by the Axis powers. Slogans such as sovereignty and non-intervention are still invoked by Soviet spokesmen in arguments against proposals that would interfere with Communist control of certain countries, particularly in Eastern Europe, or that would introduce any measure of outside inspection or supervision over what is taking place in these countries. The principles of sovereignty and territorial inviolability also serve to strengthen the ideological defenses of the Soviet Union and its allies against intrusions for reconnaissance and other hostile purposes.

Offensively, some of these slogans, particularly those of self-determination and equality, have long been utilized in Communist propaganda to undermine the power of the stronger "capitalist" states in their colonies and spheres of influence. One of the first acts of the Soviet regime was to renounce extraterritorial privileges which Imperial Russia had obtained from Asian nations. Soviet spokesmen continue to emphasize anti-colonialism. In 1962, Tunkin asserted: "Modern international law is anti-colonial in its direction."[62A]

The legal content of "peaceful coexistence," an important recent addition to the Soviet armory of "new principles of international law," is suggested in the 1961 Program of the Communist Party of the Soviet Union:

> *Peaceful coexistence* implies renunciation of war as a means of settling international disputes, and their solution by negotiation; equality, mutual understanding and trust between countries; consideration for each other's interests; non-interference in internal affairs; recognition of the right of every people to solve all the problems of their country by themselves; strict respect for the sovereignty and territorial integrity of all countries; promotion of economic and cultural co-operation on the basis of complete equality and mutual benefit.[63A]

[62A] *Ibid.*, p. 11. This is elaborated in Kozhevnikov, ed., *op. cit.* (1964), pp. 121-154.

[63A] As translated in J. F. Triska, ed., *Soviet Communism: Programs and Rules* (San Francisco, Chandler, 1962), pp. 65-66.

Soviet jurists, in discussing the legal content of "peaceful coexistence," elaborate the elements listed in the Program.[64] According to the Soviet view, "peaceful coexistence" is a principle that applies only in the relations of socialist states with the non-socialist world. In the relations between the socialist states themselves, another and "higher" principle—that of "socialist (or proletarian) internationalism"—governs.[65]

The Soviet tendency is to use the term "peaceful coexistence" to belabor any policy detrimental to Soviet interests, such as restrictions on trade with the Soviet Union and other Communist countries or support of anti-Soviet movements in these countries, and to justify Soviet policies.[66] Many Western jurists fear that "peaceful coexistence" is a means by which the Soviets will attempt to direct the development of international law to the detriment of the West. As Tunkin points out, the 1961 Program of the Communist Party declares that "peaceful coexistence serves as a basis for the peaceful competition between socialism and capitalism on an international scale and constitutes *a specific form of class struggle between them*." He adds that "in upholding the international law principles of peaceful coexistence and using them to support their foreign policy, the socialist states are striving for the constant strengthening of the positions of the world socialist system in its competition with capitalism." [67] Another important "new principle" of international

[64] The most extensive treatment is in G. P. Zadorozhnyi, *Mirnoie Sosushchestvovaniie i Mezhdunarodnoie Pravo* (Moscow, Izdatel'stvo "Mezhdunarodnye Otnosheniia," 1964).

[65] The Yugoslav leaders reject this view, insisting that "peaceful coexistence" applies also in the relations between socialist states. See J. N. Hazard, "Coexistence, Co-operation, and the Common Law," in E. McWhinney, ed., *Law, Foreign Policy, and the East-West Détente* (Toronto, University of Toronto Press, 1964), p. 22.

[66] See, for example, F. A. Korovin, "Ustav OON i Mirnoie Sosushchestvovanie," *Soviet Yearbook of International Law*, 1961 (Moscow, Publishing House, Academy of Sciences of USSR), p. 28.

[67] Tunkin, "XXII S'ezd KPSS . . . ", *op. cit.*, p. 12. Emphasis added.

[68] G. I. Tunkin, *Voprosy Teorii Mehzdunarodnogo Prava* (Moscow, Gosudarstevennoie Izdatel'stvo Yuridicheskoi Literatury, 1962), p. 54. (Tunkin's book has been published in a French translation: G. I. Tunkin, *Droit International Public: Problèmes Théoriques* (Paris, A. Pedone, 1965). See also Koshevnikov, ed., *op. cit.* (1964), p. 596.

law which is allegedly in the process of being established is that of "general and complete disarmament"—a well-known tenet of current Soviet foreign policy.[68]

Another example of Soviet use of international law doctrines of uncertain content has been the reiteration of the notion that "unequal" treaties are invalid *ab initio*.[69] According to the standard Soviet textbook of international law:

> Equal treaties are treaties concluded on the basis of the equality of the parties; unequal treaties are those which do not fulfill this elementary requirement. Unequal treaties are not legally binding; equal treaties must be strictly observed.[70]

This alleged norm of international law can be easily manipulated by Soviet spokesmen to deny the binding force of treaties that do not accord with Soviet interests and to impress the weaker nations which have long resented certain of their treaties with stronger states.[71] The 1964 textbook asserts that valid treaties are those based on the principles of sovereign equality, mutual advantage, and free manifestation of the wills of the parties, but appears to stress absence of coercion.[72]

The more specific and technical norms are often reinterpreted and applied flexibly to strengthen Soviet positions and weaken those of opponents. International law, however, is also useful to the Soviet Union, as it is to other states, in preventing excessive friction with the outside world and in facilitating such relations of a cooperative nature with the

---

69 In contrast to the doctrine of *rebus sic stantibus*, which bases the invalidity of the treaty on subsequent changes in circumstances. See p. 42.

70 English translation from Academy of Sciences of the USSR . . . , *International Law, op. cit.*, p. 248. A Soviet representative in the United Nations stated that "treaties were valid only when based on equality of rights, mutual advantage, and due respect for the interests of the parties." United Nations Doc. A/C. 6/SR. 738, 12 Oct. 1962.

71 See, for example, V. M. Shurshalov, *Osnovaniia Deistvitel'nosti Mezhdunardonykh Dogovorov* (Moscow, Izdatel'stvo Akademii Nauk SSSR, 1957), pp. 152-153, where the Soviet author declares "unequal" the agreements concluded by the United States under the Marshall Plan and Point Four programs. See, further, A. N. Talalaiev and V. G. Boiarshinov, "Neravnopravnye Dogovory kak Forma Uderzhaniia v Kolonial'noi Zavisimosti Novykh Gosudarstv Azii i Afriki," *Soviet Yearbook of International Law*, 1961, p. 156.

72 Kozhevnikov, ed., *op. cit.* (1964), pp. 321-322.

"capitalist" states as the policies of the governments concerned permit. There has been a large measure of routine compliance by the Soviet Union with the generally accepted norms in such areas as diplomatic immunities and jurisdiction on the high seas. The Soviet Union, moreover, has entered into a great number of bilateral and multilateral treaties and agreements with non-Communist states. A recent comprehensive study shows that in the first forty years of its existence (1917-1957) the Soviet state entered into 2,516 treaties and agreements, and the tendency appears to be toward an increase in Soviet treaty obligations and relationships.[73] Only a small proportion of these treaties and agreements have been primarily political in character. Most have been in the functional areas of world affairs—trade, communications, transport, consular relations, health, conservation of natural resources (such as certain stocks of fish, seals, and whales). In these areas, Communist and non-Communist states have often deemed it mutually advantageous, if only temporarily, to cooperate with each other, and international law has provided the framework for the desired cooperation.[74]

Impact on Universality

Has the distinctive Soviet attitude toward international law served to reduce the scope of universally recognized international law and its role in world affairs?

Verbally, the Soviet Union seems to attach great importance to international law. In an address to a domestic audi-

---

[73] J. F. Triska and R. M. Slusser, *The Theory, Law, and Policy of Soviet Treaties* (Stanford, Univ. Press, 1962), p. 4.

[74] Those who regard the cold war as a bar to the application of international law between the two sides may be surprised to learn that the country which has made the greatest number of treaties with the Soviet Union is the United States. Of the 373 instruments to which both the United States and the USSR have been parties for varying periods between 1917 and 1957, only some 80 were bilateral; the others were multilateral. See Triska and Slusser, *op. cit.*, pp. 4-5; see also R. M. Slusser and J. F. Triska, *A Calendar of Soviet Treaties 1917-1957* (Stanford, Univ. Press, 1959), pp. 526-528. In 1963, the U.S. Department of State listed 128 treaties and agreements as being in force between the two states. *Congressional Record*, Vol. 109, Part 13, p. 17827 (24 Sept. 1963).

ence on 30 August 1959, shortly before his trip to the United States which culminated in the Camp David meeting with President Eisenhower, Chairman Khrushchev said:

> We are deeply conscious that without the observance of the norms of international law, without the fulfilment of undertakings assumed in relations between states, there can be no trust, and without trust there can be no peaceful coexistence.[75]

Soviet jurists affirm the existence of a general international law binding on all states. Indeed, to deny the existence of such international law would be to deprive Soviet foreign policy of a useful tool for struggle and cooperation with other states. Tunkin refers to a new "socialist" international law, regulating the relations between the states of the "socialist camp," which is in the process of formation and which is based on the principle of "proletarian internationalism." Nevertheless, he asserts that "socialist" norms, which operate only between the "socialist" states, are supplementary to, and not inconsistent with, general international law.[76] The insistence that there are special "socialist" norms, however, tends to limit the scope and importance of general international law, although some of these special norms, contained primarily in treaties between the socialist states, are seen, on examination, to follow in large part the patterns of provisions in treaties between the USSR and "capitalist" states.[77]

Yet the universality of international law seemingly recognized by the Soviet jurists falls short of the traditional Western concept of universality. First, Soviet jurists claim for the Soviet state the right to pick and choose among the norms of international law. Tunkin advances what he calls "the new

---

[75] *Pravda*, 1 Sept. 1959. This statement was often quoted by Soviet jurists while Khrushchev was in office.

[76] Tunkin, "XXII S'ezd KPSS . . . ," *op. cit.*, p. 14, and *Voprosy Teorii Mezhdunarodnogo Prava*, *op. cit.*, pp. 325-327; also Tunkin, "Mirnoie Sosushchestvovanie i Mezhdunarodnoie Pravo," *Sovetskoie Gosudarstvo i Pravo*, No. 7 (1956). For latest elaborations, see Kozhevnikov, ed., *op cit.* (1964), pp. 94-120, and M. E. Ayrapetian and V. V. Sukhodeiev, *Novyi Tip Mezhdunarodnykh Otnoshenii* (Moscow, Izdatel'stvo "Mysl'"), 1964), pp. 223-241.

[77] See J. N. Hazard, "Soviet Socialism as a Public Order System," *Proceedings of the American Society of International Law* (1959), p. 30.

doctrine of agreement"—the view that general international law which is mutually binding on states belonging to the "two existing systems" (capitalist and socialist) is composed only of norms accepted by agreement between them. Such agreement may be express (in the form of treaties) or tacit (in the form of custom).[78] From the Soviet point of view, there is nothing "new" in Tunkin's "doctrine of agreement." From Korovin on, Soviet jurists have sought to claim for the Soviet state the freedom to reject those norms of international law that are not acceptable to it. This position, without destroying the principle of universality, tends to narrow the scope of general international law and to retard its growth. Actually, Soviet writers for the most part refrain from specifying the norms rejected by the Soviet state, thus leaving their government freedom of action. In the past, they have merely cited, by way of example, "unequal" treaties, the League Mandates System, and certain obsolescent ceremonial practices.[79] In general, the Soviet government seems to prefer to deny that certain norms of traditional international law ever gained general acceptance, and to reinterpret other norms, rather than to reject them outright.[80]

Perhaps even more important is the Soviet emphasis on the creation of "new principles." Although the idea of a "new international law" is not confined to Soviet writers and spokesmen, the Soviet insistence that a general international

[78] G. I. Tunkin, "Co-existence and International Law," *Recueil des Cours*, Vol. 95 (1958-III), p. 1. See also, his "Remarks on the Juridical Nature of Customary Norms of International Law," *California Law Review*, Vol. 49, No. 3 (Aug. 1961), p. 419; and Kozhevnikov, ed., *op. cit.* (1964), p. 56. Soviet jurists, without rejecting custom as a source of international law, have always emphasized treaties as the most important source. It is apparent that the Soviet State is interested in de-emphasizing the role of customary law, which in the main was developed before the Soviet regime was created and in the shaping of which the latter had little part. Triska and Slusser, *The Theory, Law, and Policy of Soviet Treaties, op. cit.*, pp. 9-31. For a similar reason, Soviet jurists generally reject the prevalent Western view that certain principles found in various national systems of law may be applied by analogy in international law as "general principles of law." For the latest presentation of the Soviet view of the "sources" of international law, see Kozhevnikov, ed., *op. cit.* (1954), pp. 41-49.

[79] See, for example, Akademiia Nauk SSSR, Institut Prava, *Mezhdunarodnoie Pravo* (Moscow, Gosudarstvennoie Izdatel'stvo Yuridicheskoi Literatury, 1951), p. 12.

law of substantially new content is being developed under Soviet influence, and that even "general and complete disarmament" is becoming part of it, weakens the consensus of states on which international law must be based if it is to be truly universal. In varying degrees, the Western states have been reluctant to accept generalities such as "self-determination," "anti-colonialism," and "peaceful coexistence," let alone "general and complete disarmament," as legal norms.

Observance in Practice

The extent to which the Soviet Union accepts international law on the verbal level is, however, not as important as the degree to which it lives up to the law on the level of action. There is a widespread impression in the West that the USSR has been completely heedless of the norms of international law, and, in particular, that it has no compunctions about disregarding or repudiating its treaty obligations whenever convenient. At times, a stark contrast is drawn between what is assumed to be the law-abiding behavior of the Western states and the lawlessness of the Soviet Union. Long lists of alleged treaty violations by the Soviet Union have been compiled by official sources in the United States.[81]

---

[80] See, for example, G. E. Vilkov, *Natsionalizatsiia i Mezhdunarodnoie Pravo* (Moscow, Izdatel'stvo IMO, 1962), pp. 75-91, and G. I. Tunkin, "Problema Mezhdunarodno-Pravovoi Otvetstvennosti Gosudarstva v Kommissii Mezhdunarodnogo Prava OON," *Soviet Yearbook of International Law, 1960*, p. 92, denying the existence of a generally accepted "international standard" of treatment of aliens; A. N. Nikolayev, *Problema Territorial'nykh Vod v Mezhdunarodnom Prave* (Moscow, Gosudarstvennoie Izdatel'stvo Yuridicheskoi Literatury, 1954), pp. 40-41, denying that the three-mile limit of territorial waters is a generally accepted norm. Representing the Soviet Union in the Assembly's Sixth Committee, Tunkin declared that "the USSR did not recognize all the previously existing rules of international law," but specified as being rejected by the Soviet Union only certain Czarist Russian treaties and "the system of capitulations and consular jurisdiction in the countries of the Orient." GAOR: 16th Sess., 6th Cmtte., 717th Mtg., 21 Nov. 1961, para. 15.

[81] See, for example, "Soviet Violations of Treaties and Agreements," U. S. Department of State *Bulletin*, Vol. 23, No. 574 (3 July 1950), p. 8; U. S. Senate, Committee on the Judiciary, *Soviet Political Agreements and Results*, 84th Cong., 2nd. Sess., Sen. Doc. No. 125 (1956). For a more objective compilation by the U.S. Department of State, see *Congressional Record*, Vol. 109, Part 13, p. 17827 (24 Sept. 1963).

But the reality is more complex than simplistic contrasts between Western and Soviet behavior. Mutual charges of violations of treaties and other norms of interstate relations are as old as history. Even the most legal-minded Western nations have at times admittedly violated international law.[82] It would be extremely difficult, if not impossible, for any impartial scholar or group of scholars to determine and compare the frequency with which various states have, in different periods of history, violated international law. The most basic difficulty arises from the very nature of legal norms. Legal scholars increasingly recognize that no legal norm, whether expressed in writing in a treaty or not, is "plain" and admits of only one interpretation. In varying degrees, all norms have a rubber-like quality which permits them to be reinterpreted to fit new needs and conditions and renders almost hopeless the task of an "objective" interpreter.

The difficulties of determining and comparing violations of the customary norms of international law are even greater because of the controversial nature of many such norms. For example, many norms governing the validity and termination of treaties, including the doctrine of *rebus sic stantibus,* are still unsettled and subject to doubt. Judges of the highest courts, including the International Court of Justice, often disagree in their interpretation of the law, even though they have the advantages of adversary proceedings and the production of all available evidence as to the intended meaning of a norm and as to the facts of the alleged violation. There is the further difficulty of assessing the relative importance of treaty violations. Is a minor breach of one of the numerous provisions in a treaty of commerce to be given the same weight as the open repudiation of a major political undertaking? Serious scholars have therefore refrained from passing

---

[82] See O. J. Lissitzyn, "Western and Soviet Perspectives on International Law— A Comparison," *Proceedings of the American Society of International Law* (1959), p. 21.

[83] For example, Triska and Slusser, *The Theory, Law, and Policy of Soviet Treaties, op. cit.,* p. 389. On the significance of differences in the degrees of breaches of international law, see R. A. Falk, *op. cit.,* p. 250.

definitive judgments on the frequency of treaty violations by the Soviet Union.[83]

Yet a legal norm, like a rubber band, cannot be stretched *ad infinitum* without being broken. An impartial observer, however cautious, is likely to share the impression that violations of international law, including that of treaties, by the Soviet Union have been relatively frequent, particularly in matters of high political importance. Furthermore, there is a widely shared impression that it is precisely the principles most loudly proclaimed by Soviet spokesmen—those of sovereignty, territorial inviolability, non-aggression, non-intervention, and self-determination—that have been most flagrantly disregarded by the Soviet Union in its relations with states such as Finland, the Baltic republics, Poland, and Hungary. Soviet pledges not to support subversive activities in other countries, embodied in many treaties and agreements, have proved to be unreliable.[84] Soviet manipulation of the norms of international law to justify and implement Soviet policy has been so unrestrained and often seemingly so oblivious of the requirements of reciprocity and consistency as to create an impression, particularly in the Western countries, of cynicism and lack of good faith.

As already noted, however, there has also been much routine observance of international law by the Soviet Union. Despite minor incidents, diplomatic immunities have generally been observed well enough to enable the Soviet Union to maintain diplomatic intercourse with the western world. "Capitalist" and Soviet-bloc vessels ply the seas in mutual reliance on the principle of freedom of the seas. The Soviet claim of a twelve-mile zone of territorial waters, which may be traced to pre-Soviet anxieties about Russia's long coastline and weak navy, is not unique in the contemporary world and has not prevented the maintenance of a large measure of universal public order at sea. The Soviet Union has, in the

---

[84] Triska and Slusser, *op. cit.*, pp. 394-395.
[85] *Ibid.*

main, lived up to its commitments under a large number of technical, economic, and other functional treaties.[85]

The observance by the Soviet Union of much of international law need not be a cause for surprise. It demonstrates the essential role international law still plays even in the relations between antagonistic states so long as there is no all-out military conflict. International relations simply cannot be maintained without a framework of mutually recognized and observed norms. The sanction for persistent non-observance of these norms is interruption or impairment of the mutually desired relationships regulated by them. This sanction operates with respect to the Soviet Union as well as to the "capitalist" states.

Considerations of reciprocity, moreover, sometimes induce the Soviet Union to bring its practice into closer conformity with that in the rest of the world. An example is the modification effected in 1956 in Soviet law and practice on diplomatic immunities. Under regulations enacted in 1927,[86] full immunities were extended in the USSR only to foreign personnel with the rank of diplomatic officer and denied to subordinate administrative and service personnel, such as clerks and servants. Certain other countries, including France and Switzerland, made similar distinctions. But in the United Kingdom, the United States, and most other nations, administrative and service personnel, with certain exceptions, enjoyed full diplomatic immunities. To rectify this imbalance, the British Diplomatic Immunities Restriction Act, 1955, empowered the British government to withdraw certain immunities from personnel of the diplomatic mission of a state to the extent that the personnel of the British diplomatic mission in that state were denied similar immunities. This power was used to restrict the immunities of subordinate Soviet personnel in London. Shortly thereafter, a Soviet decree provided that diplomatic immunities might be accord-

---

86 See A. H. Feller and M. O. Hudson, *A Collection of the Diplomatic and Consular Laws and Regulations of Various Countries* (Washington, Carnegie Endowment for International Peace, 1933), Vol. 2, p. 1218.

ed to the "technical and service" personnel of foreign diplomatic missions (with the exception of Soviet citizens) on a basis of reciprocity. The British Government thereupon restored the immunities of Soviet personnel.[87]

The Soviets, moreover, do not always persist in maintaining clearly untenable legal positions, as shown by the modification of the Soviet attitude toward the effect of reservations to multilateral treaties. In 1950-51, in the United Nations General Assembly debates and the proceedings before the International Court of Justice concerning reservations to the Genocide Convention, the USSR argued that any state could become a party to a general multilateral treaty with any reservation it wished, regardless of the consent of other parties. This position was so untenable that by 1958 it had been quietly modified by the important qualification that a party objecting to a reservation need not regard itself as bound by the treaty with respect to the reserving state.[88] The effect of reservations remains an unsettled issue in international law, but the new Soviet position is very similar to the so-called Pan American Rule which appears to have gained considerable support in recent years.[89]

Elements of Divergence

The limiting influence of the Communist attitude toward international law has been particularly evident with respect

---

[87] For the 1955 Restriction Act, see 4 Eliz. 2, c. 21, 21 Dec. 1955; for the implementing Order in Council, see the Diplomatic Immunities Restriction Order, 1956, *Statutory Instruments*, No. 84, 25 Jan. 1956; for the Soviet decree, see Ukase of 27 Mar. 1956, reprinted in Institut Mezhdunarodnykh Otnoshenii, *Mezhdunarodnoie Pravo v Izbrannykh Dokumentakh* (Moscow, Izdatel'stvo IMO, 1957), p. 26; for the restoration of immunities in London, see Diplomatic Immunities Restriction (Amendment) Order, 1956 *Statutory Instruments*, No. 1579, 15 Oct. 1956. A similar reciprocal arrangement was reported to have been made between Moscow and Washington: see G. I. Tunkin, "Some Developments in International Law Concerning Diplomatic Privileges and Immunities," *International Affairs* (Moscow), No. 12 (1957), p. 70.

[88] Triska and Slusser, *The Theory, Law, and Policy of Soviet Treaties, op. cit.*, pp. 83-84; W. Bishop, Jr., "Reservations to Treaties," *Recueil des Cours*, Vol. 103 (1961-II), p. 245, and pp. 84-88.

[89] See p. 89.

to the use of adjudication as a means of settlement of international disputes. Soviet leaders have generally taken a negative attitude toward all proposals to refer such disputes to the International Court of Justice or to arbitration. They have rejected, for example, the repeated offers of the United States to submit to the Court the disputes growing out of the shooting down of United States military aircraft by Soviet forces. The Soviet Union has opposed all attempts to extend the compulsory jurisdiction of the Court and has never accepted such jurisdiction under the "optional clause" of Article 36 of the Court's Statute. It has generally tried to minimize resort to the advisory function of the Court by the United Nations.

The picture, to be sure, is not all black and white. A majority of the members of the United Nations have not submitted to the jurisdiction of the Court under the "optional clause," and many of the others have hedged their submission with far-reaching reservations. The United States has made its submission virtually nugatory by the "Connally Amendment," and other Western powers have not distinguished themselves by strong leadership in favor of making greater use of the Court.

Soviet leaders, moreover, have not been completely inflexible in their opposition to international adjudication. The Soviet Union has become a party to several multilateral treaties, such as the Constitution of the International Labour Organisation, which provide for the submission of disputes arising under them to the Court. In 1947, it acquiesced (by abstention) in the recommendation of the United Nations Security Council that the United Kingdom and Albania refer to the Court their dispute growing out of incidents in the Corfu Channel. On several occasions in its history, for example, in controversies with the United Kingdom in 1923 and 1924, the Soviet government vainly suggested resort to arbitration or third-party decision.[90] The peace treaties of 1947 with Italy and the other European allies of Nazi Ger-

62

many provided for arbitral tribunals (under the name of conciliation commissions) to pass on certain property and other claims of nationals of the victorious powers, including the USSR. In the spring of 1962, the USSR supported in the Security Council a Cuban proposal that the International Court of Justice be requested to render an advisory opinion on the legality of the exclusion of the government of Cuba from the Organization of American States. It was the United States and its friends that defeated this proposal.

Yet the fact remains that, in general, the influence of the Soviet bloc has been strongly exerted against the extension of the judicial function in the international community. This is but one manifestation of the deep-seated influence of Communist ideology on the Soviet attitude toward the role of law in world affairs. In a world divided into two hostile camps, there can be no "impartial" judges. Maxim Litvinov put it graphically in 1922:

> It was necessary to face the fact that there was not one world but two—a Soviet world and a non-Soviet world . . . there was no third world to arbitrate. . . . Only an angel could be unbiased in judging Russian affairs.[91]

In a world in which the Communist nations are still in a minority, they cannot afford to entrust their interests to the decision of a body in which the rule of unanimity does not apply.

Indeed, if one posits a world split into two fundamentally hostile camps—and an inevitable victory for the "socialist camp"—international relations cannot be based on genuine trust or wholehearted cooperation. Coexistence, according

---

90 J. Degras, ed., *Soviet Documents on Foreign Policy* (London, Oxford Univ. Press, 1951), Vol. 1, pp. 390, 473. In 1923 the Soviet government also suggested arbitration of the question of authenticity of documents made public by the United States Government which indicated Soviet involvement in Communist activities in the United States. *The New York Times*, 22 Dec. 1923; see also, Ministerstvo Inostrannykh Del SSSR, *Dokumenty . . ., op. cit.*, Vol. 6 (1962), p. 552, and A. M. Ladyzhenskii and I. P. Blishchenko, *Mirnye Sredstva Razresheniia Sporov mezhdu Gosudarstvami* (Moscow, Gosudarstvennoie Izadel'stvo Yuridicheskoi Literatury, 1962), pp. 112-113.

91 Quoted in Taracouzio, *op. cit.*, p. 296.

to the Soviet view, is bound to be transitory. Cooperation is but a form of struggle. This view is self-fulfilling; it creates hostility and mistrust on the other side, and thus seems to confirm the Communist doctrine of implacable antagonism. In such an atmosphere, a genuine common effort to extend the rule of law in world affairs is hardly possible. In a world moving in the direction of a basic social transformation, moreover, the sense of the long-term advantages of stability and good faith on which international law in the West has largely rested is attenuated.[92]

In the West, self-interest as the motive for the observance of international law is sometimes reinforced by a sense of moral obligation. Observance of the law is a symbol of rectitude. For a good Communist, however, the moral obligation to observe the law cannot be a legitimate consideration. There is no evidence that the Soviet leaders of today have given up the Leninist conception of morality, which was tersely summed up in 1955 in these words: "Marxism-Leninism sees the supreme criterion of Communist morality in the struggle for communism." [93]

Another factor in the Soviet attitude toward international law and its role, distinct from but related to Communist ideology, is the nature of the Soviet system of public order. Two features of this system are relevant here: the direct control of virtually all economic activity by the state, and the authoritarian control of the population by the government.

As already pointed out, the development of international law in the West has been in part due to the needs of private persons carrying on economic activity across national boundaries. These needs, which often find expression in pressures exercised by private interest groups on their governments,

92 For the influence of ideology on Soviet foreign policy, see Z. K. Brzezinski, *Ideology and Power in Soviet Politics* (New York, Praeger, 1962), pp. 102-113; A. Dallin, *The Soviet Union at the United Nations* (New York, Praeger, 1962), pp. 3-12, 182-189.

93 A. Shishkin, *Osnovy Kommunisticheskoi Morali* (Moscow, Gosudarstvennoie Izdatel'stvo Politicheskoi Literatury, 1955), p. 95, as translated in R. C. Tucker, *Philosophy and Myth in Karl Marx* (Cambridge, Univ. Press, 1961), pp. 13-14n.

not only serve to strengthen the role of international law in governmental policies, but also require the services of an influential group of professional men and women—the lawyers—who have an occupational interest in the existence and maintenance of the rule of law. Their influence strengthens the "law habit" which in turn reinforces other factors making for the continued observance of international law. Moreover, in open societies, public opinion can sometimes be mobilized in criticism of violations by governments of international law.

In the Soviet Union and other Communist states, the factor of private economic interest in the development and observance of international law is absent. Lawyers have little influence on governmental policy and rarely rise to the top levels of official and party hierarchy. As yet, little that can be called a "law habit" is apparent on the Soviet scene. The absence of private economic activity has, moreover, directly affected the Soviet position on a number of important issues in international law. The Soviet state economy was founded on wholesale confiscation of private property—Russian and foreign—and Soviet spokesmen continue to uphold the view that a state may expropriate without compensation the private property of foreign nationals within its territory.[94] This view is at sharp variance with the legal position and the interests of countries with highly developed private enterprise. In the Soviet Union, foreign trade, like most other economic activities, is a state monopoly, and the Soviet Union has therefore stoutly upheld the traditional "absolute" doctrine of sovereign immunity of a state from the jurisdiction of foreign courts. By contrast, in the West, partly as a reaction to the rise of "state trading," there has been a tendency to adopt a "restrictive" view of sovereign immunity, which would deny immunity to a foreign state in suits arising from

[94] See, for example, sources cited in note 80; also, the remarks of the Soviet representative, United Nations Doc. A/C.2/SR.834, 15 Nov. 1962, p. 16.
[95] For the Soviet point of view, see M. M. Boguslavskii, *Immunitet Gosudarstva* (Moscow, Izdatel'stvo IMO, 1962). In many commercial agreements, however, the Soviet Union has consented to limit its immunity.

its commercial activities.[95] In this matter, the Soviet Union thus clings to a conservative legal doctrine, while the West appears as an innovator.

It would be an oversimplification to say that every utterance of Soviet jurists is dictated by the government. In fact, disagreement among them on technical points is frequent. Even on such a seemingly important question as the continuity of the Russian Empire and the Soviet state as a single subject of international law, there has been persistent disagreement among Soviet writers. Similarly, there is a continuing controversy over the question whether international organizations, in particular the United Nations, are to be regarded as subjects of international law. Disagreement on more fundamental issues, such as the proper explanation of the existence of international law in terms of Marxist doctrine, has also occurred. At the height of the post-Stalin "thaw," some voices were even raised in defense of the concept of natural law and natural rights, which is usually rejected by Soviet jurists.[96] It would be a mistake, therefore, to attribute to the Soviet government every view on international law expressed by every Soviet writer. The government, it may be surmised, seeks to retain freedom of argument, particularly on some of the more technical points of international law, by not approving or disapproving the views found in "unofficial" Soviet literature until the concrete necessity for taking a position arises. But Soviet writers are not expected to express an opinion contrary to officially adopted doctrine or policy. No Soviet jurist has admitted that the USSR has ever violated international law.

---

[96] For Soviet views on state succession, see M. M. Avakov, *Pravopreiemstvo Sovetskogo Gosudarstva* (Moscow, Gosudarstvennoie Izdatel'stvo Yuridicheskoi Literatury, 1961); N. V. Zakharova, "O Mezhdunarodnoi Pravosub'ektnosti Gosudarstva pri Sotsial'noi Revoliutsii," *Soviet Yearbook of International Law, 1960*, p. 157. R. L. Bobrov, "O Pravovoi Prirode Organizatsii Ob'edienennykh Natsii," *ibid., 1959*, p. 229; and G. E. Zhvaniia and L. A. Aleksidze, *Ibid., 1958*, pp. 520, 523, deal, respectively, with international organization and natural law. For the prevalent Soviet view on natural law, see, for example, G. P. Zhukov, *Kritika Estestvennopravovykh Teorii Mezhdunarodnogo Prava* (Moscow, Gosudarstvennoie Izdatel'stvo Yuridicheskoi Literatury, 1961).

The nature of Soviet public order inhibits free contacts between Soviet citizens, including international lawyers, and the outside world. This makes for a sense of continuing estrangement and lack of genuine understanding of the ideas current in the West. In addition, the Soviet predilection for secrecy inhibits the government from entering into certain types of treaty commitments. For example, the failure of the USSR to adhere to the Chicago Convention on International Civil Aviation and thus become a member of the International Civil Aviation Organization (ICAO) can only be explained by the provisions in the Convention for the admission of foreign civil aircraft on non-commercial, non-scheduled flights, and for the reporting by member states of the traffic and financial statistics of their airlines.[97] Soviet fear of observation by reconnaissance satellites impedes efforts to reach agreement on the law of outer space. The emphasis on secrecy is an important obstacle to the acceptance by the USSR of international inspection which is essential to an agreement for disarmament. The desire of Soviet leaders to control the population without outside interference is also reflected in the unanimously expressed view of Soviet jurists that individuals can have no rights in international law.

Some observers have sought to trace the limiting and distorting effects of the cold war on international law to "bipolarity" in the structure of world politics.[98] However, the Soviet estrangement from the outside world and from traditional concepts of international law did not begin with the rise of the USSR to its present power position. It began with the establishment of the Communist regime in Russia and was evident in the inter-war period even when the Soviet state was relatively weak. The growth of Soviet power and "bipolarity," however, has accentuated a pre-existing challenge to world public order. In such a situation, the interest

[97] Cf. Kozhevnikov, ed., *op. cit.* (1964), p. 250.
[98] See M. A. Kaplan and N. de B. Katzenbach, *op. cit., passim;* J. J. G. Syatauw, *Some Newly Established Asian States and the Development of International Law* (The Hague, Nijhoff, 1961), pp. 4-9.

in strict observance of the law is particularly likely to be subordinated to considerations of national security.

Nor is the Soviet challenge a product of the "Russian" tradition. The Russian Empire, like other great powers, played the game of power politics and imperialism. At times, like other states, it violated or misused international law. But its existence and policies created no sense of a "crisis" in international law; its economic and social institutions, though somewhat backward and marred by religious discrimination, were basically similar to those of the West. Russia had no distinctive doctrine of international law and participated freely in the legal life of the international community.

Perspectives

Despite the impact of Communist ideology and system of public order on international law and despite widespread distrust of Soviet motives and promises, "capitalist" countries, including the United States, continue to negotiate and conclude agreements with the USSR. Such agreements are based not on "mutual trust," but on recognition of common or mutual interests and the expectation that self-interest will induce both sides to honor their commitments.[99] International law can also play an important role in the maintenance of the strength and cohesion of the non-Communist world, particularly as a framework for the existence, evolution, and functions of international organizations of world-wide or regional character, and as a technique for avoidance of friction.

It is clear, however, that Communist ideology and public order stand in the way of the gradual evolution of mankind toward the rule of law in world affairs. Is there any prospect for a significant change? The short answer is that no ideology or system of public order is immutable. As Harold D. Lass-

---

[99] See, e.g., George C. McGhee, "East-West Relations Today," U.S. Department of State *Bulletin*, Vol. 50, No. 1292 (30 March 1964), p. 488.

well has said, "the doctrines of any political system are open to changes of many kinds, particularly in the intensity with which they are held and the specific interpretations to which they give rise." [100] The threat of nuclear devastation has already induced the Soviet leaders to abandon the doctrine of inevitability of war between the "capitalist" and the "socialist" states. Serious differences of ideology and policy have already developed between the various Communist parties. The attitudes of the leaders of these parties toward international law appear to reflect these differences, from the relative moderation of the Yugoslav government at one end of the spectrum to the intransigence of the Communist regime in mainland China at the other.[101] Even the latter, however, like the Soviet government in its early days, invokes international law in protest against actions contrary to its interests and follows traditional precepts in matters such as diplomatic immunities.

It is possible, therefore, that if coexistence between the Soviet bloc and the "capitalist" world continues, and if the West maintains a healthy growth rate in all fields of human endeavor, the objective necessities of international life, the cumulative effect of cultural and other exchanges between the two, the disappearance of hostility-breeding feelings of inferiority with the succession of generations, and a breakdown in the unity of the "socialist camp," will bring about a

---

[100] "Introduction: Universality versus Parochialism," in M. S. McDougal and F. P. Feliciano, *Law and Minimum World Public Order: the Legal Regulation of International Coercion* (New Haven, Yale Univ. Press, 1961), pp. xxii-xxiii. For reinterpretation of the Moslem doctrine of international relations, at one time as intransigent as that of the Communists, see the addresses of Majid Khadduri and R. K. Ramazani in *Proceedings of the American Society of International Law* (1959), pp. 49, 53.

[101] For Yugoslav attitudes toward international law, see E. Dorsch, *Der gegenwärtige Stand der Jugoslawischen Völkerrechtslehre,* Studien des Institus für Ostrecht, Vol. 11 (Herrenalb, Verlag für Internationalen Kulturaustausch, 1960); for indications of Communist Chinese attitudes, see the report of a discussion by Chinese jurists at Shanghai in 1958, *Soviet Yearbook of International Law, 1958,* p. 544; also, T'iao Yueh, "A Preliminary Appraisal of Bourgeois Concept of International Law," *Kuo-Chi Wen-T'i Yen-Chiu* (Peking), 3 July 1959, as translated in *Union Research Service* (Hong Kong), Vol. 16. No. 21 (11 Sept. 1959). A comparative study of the attitudes of Communist elites toward international law remains to be made.

gradual reinterpretation of Soviet doctrines to permit international law to play a greater role in the affairs of mankind. The Soviet "two-camp" image of the world is beginning to fade. The partial nuclear test-ban treaty, with France and Communist China as the major non-participants, cuts across both "camps." There are signs that in the development of space law and some other matters in which joint American-Soviet leadership is evident the "two-camp" concept also does not apply.

The process of reinterpretation of Communist ideology is likely to be furthered by the participation of Communist and "capitalist" nations in joint or cooperative activities, such as the exploration and development of Antarctica and outer space, as well as by an intensification of cultural and other exchanges in all fields and at all levels. International law, in turn, facilitates such activities and exchanges.

The prospect is not for a sudden leap from anarchy into a world ruled by law, but for a very gradual erosion of the extreme hostility to other systems of public order implicit in Communist ideology and for a concomitant gradual expansion of the role of international law in the relations between the two camps. (However, the Chinese Communist elite, which has come to power more recently than the Soviet elite, which rules a country less advanced economically and scientifically than the Soviet Union, and which has been excluded from the activities of international organizations, is likely to remain at a peak of militancy and hostility toward the non-Communist world for a longer period than the Soviet elite).

It has been suggested, furthermore, that in the relations between the two power blocs led by the United States and the Soviet Union there are developing new "rules of the game" which were applied in the Cuban crisis of 1962. These rules are not cast in the technical language of international law and many jurists would deny their legal character. But it may be recalled that in the past the concepts of balance of power and "the Concert of Europe" were regarded by many as parts of "the public law of Europe," although they were not applied as technical legal norms. The new "rules," however, may fall by the wayside if the blocs continue to disintegrate and polycentrism replaces bipolarity.[102]

[102] E. McWhinney, *"Peaceful Coexistence" and Soviet-Western International Law* (Leyden, A. W. Sythoff, 1964), pp. 72-126; see also R. A. Falk, *op. cit.*, p. 262.

THE LESS DEVELOPED NATIONS

THE ATTITUDES of the newly independent and other less developed nations and their leaders toward international law cannot be identified and described as easily as those of the Soviet ruling elite. Unlike the latter, the leaders of these nations do not for the most part think and act within the framework of a single comprehensive philosophical and political system such as Marxism-Leninism. Their systems of public order, despite varying degrees of restriction on political freedom, are not as closed as those of the Communist countries and do not circumscribe with the same rigidity the freedom of expression of views on world affairs or contacts with the outside world. Within certain limits, private economic activity, private associations, and autonomous interest groups are generally permitted to exist.

The less developed nations, furthermore, differ in cultural background, levels of education, political orientation, and specific interests. Within each nation, moreover, there may be significant differences in attitudes toward international law among the various groups participating in the policy-making process. In any attempt to understand and appraise the attitudes of the developing nations, this diversity must be taken into account. Generalization is difficult. Yet many of these nations show certain common tendencies in their attitude toward international law. These tendencies are a product of resentment of past foreign domination and attitudes of superiority, and of a low level of economic development with resulting economic and technological dependence on the more advanced countries.

None of the less developed nations officially denies the existence or the binding force of international law. All have at various times invoked its norms in disputes with other

72

states and in debates in international organizations. With varying degrees of interest, they have participated in diplomatic conferences for the codification and development of international law, and in the work of the Assembly's Sixth Committee. All have entered into numerous treaties, including many general multilateral conventions, thus extending the scope of the application of international law. Several have submitted disputes to the International Court of Justice.

Current of Discontent

Yet, among the less developed nations, there is a perceptible current of discontent with traditional international law. This discontent generally does not lead to a denial or depreciation of the role of international law in world affairs. Indeed, spokesmen for the less developed countries often stress the need for the further development of international law in order to increase its importance in relations among nations. But development means change, and the desire for the development of international law in part reflects a feeling that the traditional norms are a creation of a limited number of Western states and do not necessarily serve the needs and aspirations of the less developed and, particularly, the newly independent nations. Consequently, it is felt, the traditional norms are not, or should not be, binding on them. Judge Radhabinod Pal, the Indian member of the United Nations International Law Commission, quoted and summarized views expressed in the Sixth Committee as follows:

"It could hardly be denied that the activities of the United Nations in the field of international law had failed to keep pace with the needs of a swiftly moving world."

Nor should it be forgotten, it was said, that the world legal community had expanded and that the great powers situated in a limited area of the world were no longer alone responsible for the creation of international law.

It was hoped that the progressive development of international law would bring about a greater degree of universality through the contributions and the active participation of the many new nations which had emerged on the international scene. Only then, it was said, would international law be able to play its rightful part in international affairs, and only then would it be possible to call for its strict and undeviating observance by all states.

As to the 30 to 40 new states which had arisen since the end of the First World War, it was questioned to what extent they ought to be bound by rules of international law which they had not helped to create and which very often ran counter to their interests. The formal answer, it was suggested, was very simple: when a state acceded to the international community it automatically was understood to conform to its rules and institutions. The substance of the problem was, however, declared much more complex and difficult. If numerous rules of international law did not have the active support of a large sector of the international community, the entire machinery for the peaceful solution of disputes would, it was felt, be without foundation.[103]

The discontent of the less developed nations with existing international law reflects more than the feeling that some of its norms may be outmoded or opposed to the interests of the weaker states and the newly independent states. There is also a desire to incorporate in it certain principles that have been usually regarded in the West as political rather than legal and that, by their very generality and flexibility of application, lend themselves to manipulation. The non-Western nations tend to use such general principles as weapons in their efforts to do away with the remnants of Western domination in both political and economic spheres. The concept of self-determination, for example, has been used primarily as an instrument of political pressure for the emancipation of colonies from Western rule. The Declaration on the Granting of Independence to Colonial Countries and Peoples[104] affirms that "all peoples have the right to self-

103 "Future Role of the International Law Commission in the Changing World," *United Nations Review*, Vol. 9, No. 9 (Sept. 1962), p. 31. See also *International Law in a Changing World* (Dobbs Ferry, Oceana Publications, 1963), p. 88. For a valuable symposium focussed on the attitudes and role of the new nations, see *Howard Law Review*, Vol. 8, No. 2 (Spring, 1962). An extensive bibliography is found in G. Abi-Saab, *Carnegie Endowment Conference on the Newly Independent States and International Law* (Geneva, Carnegie Endowment for International Peace, 1964), pp. 29-46.
104 General Assembly Res. 1514 (XV), 14 Dec. 1960.

determination," but is clearly directed against the remnants of Western colonialism, and has been invoked in this sense in subsequent Assembly resolutions. The idea that self-determination means the right of secession by any discontented group (for example, an ethnic minority such as the Nagas in India or the Kurds in a number of Middle Eastern states) has not been accepted. If it had, it might have served to disrupt the unity and impair the strength of many newly independent states.

Foreign Investments

"Self-determination" has also been invoked in the drive of the less developed nations for reaffirmation of their sovereignty in the economic sphere. In 1955, largely by the votes of these nations and over the opposition of many western European states, the Assembly's Third Committee adopted, for inclusion as part of Article I in both draft Covenants on Human Rights, the following provision:

> All peoples have the right of self-determination. By virtue of this right they freely determine their political status and freely pursue their economic, social and cultural development.
> The peoples may, for their own ends, freely dispose of their natural wealth and resources without prejudice to many obligations arising out of international economic co-operation, based upon the principle of mutual benefit, and international law. In no case may a people be deprived of its own means of subsistence.[105]

This formulation did not clarify the difficult problems of the legal meaning of self-determination, such as defining the "peoples" entitled to it, but it linked self-determination to the desire—already manifested on previous occasions—of the less developed states to affirm their right to dispose of their natural resources and, by implication, to limit or deemphasize

---

[105] GAOR: 10th Sess., 1955, Annexes, Agenda item 28-I (A/3077, para 77).
[106] See J. N. Hyde, "Permanent Sovereignty Over Natural Wealth and Resources." *AJIL*, Vol. 50, No. 4 (Oct. 1956), p. 854; also, General Assembly Res. 626 (VII), 21 Dec. 1952.

the right of the capital-exporting states to protect the investments of their nationals in these resources.[106]

A somewhat less extreme attitude, however, was manifest in a 1962 resolution based on the report of an Assembly Commission on Permanent Sovereignty over Natural Resources. This Commission was directed to conduct a full survey of the right of peoples and nations to "permanent sovereignty over their natural wealth and resources" which was said to be a "basic constituent of the right to self-determination." In the resolution, references to "the sovereign right" or "the inalienable right" of all states "freely to dispose of their natural wealth and resources" are balanced by declarations that "foreign investment agreements freely entered into by, or between, sovereign States shall be observed in good faith" and that, in cases of nationalization, expropriation, or requisitioning, "the owner shall be paid appropriate compensation, in accordance with the rules in force in the State taking such measures in the exercise of its sovereignty and in accordance with international law."[107] Although most of the capital-exporting states voted in favor of this resolution while the Soviet bloc abstained, the lack of definition of the requirements of international law in the matter of compensation leaves the resolution open to differing interpretations. It is, indeed, the attitude of the less developed nations toward international law norms designed for the protection of foreign nationals and their property that has caused much concern in the capital-exporting countries of the West. In the past, General Assembly resolutions on "permanent sovereignty over natural resources" have been cited in justification of nationalization measures not accompanied by what the foreign investors regarded as adequate compensation.[108]

In traditional international law there has been an "international standard" governing state responsibility for the treatment of aliens both as regards their person and their prop-

---

[107] General Assembly Res. 1314 (XIII), 12 Dec. 1958, and Res. 1803 (XVII), 14 Dec. 1962.

[108] See Hyde, *op. cit.*; also, the Soviet sources cited in note 80.

erty. Thus, in case of expropriation or nationalization, the "international standard" has required the payment of what has often been described as "prompt, adequate and effective" compensation. "Adequate" compensation has been generally defined as payment of the full value of the property, which is normally determined by the market price. The institution of diplomatic protection of nationals abroad and the "international standard" were devices by which the more advanced states sought to assure—not always successfully—security of person and property for those of their citizens who wished to invest capital, utilize skills, or otherwise do business, in the less developed parts of the world. This rule was not seriously challenged until World War I.

Subsequently, however, several seemingly coincidental historical events placed the traditional rule in jeopardy. In Russia, the new Soviet regime confiscated the private investments of foreigners as well as Russians on a vast scale and refused to pay any compensation. In Mexico, a socialist-inspired constitution adopted in 1917 paved the way for expropriation of foreign agrarian and oil properties, which gave rise to heated diplomatic controversies. In the course of the controversy concerning the expropriation of foreign-owned lands, Mexico declared that no rule of international law required payment of compensation for expropriations of "a general and impersonal" character that affected the property of citizens and aliens alike.[109] And many of the states carved out of the territory of the defeated Central Powers embarked on programs of agrarian reform that involved the redistribution of large tracts of land owned, in part, by Hungarian and German nationals.

There arose a lively debate between those who upheld the traditional "international standard" of compensation and those who sought to reduce the expropriating state's duty

[109] It should be noted, however, that in this case and in others cited below some compensation was actually paid. See p. 00. G. H. Hackworth, *Digest of International Law* (Washington, GPO, 1940-44), Vol. 3, p. 657; also, G. White, *Nationalisation of Foreign Property* (New York, Praeger, 1961), pp. 183-243.

under international law to paying foreign nationals, including business firms, the same compensation as that granted to the state's citizens. At the 1930 Hague Conference for the Codification of International Law, the doctrine that aliens were entitled to an "international standard" of treatment —implying an international duty to pay compensation independent of national laws—was upheld by the narrow margin of 23 to 17 votes. The minority, which favored the "equality of treatment" doctrine, was composed of the seven Latin American nations which took part in the vote, four Asian and African nations, five successor states of central and eastern Europe, and Portugal.[110] Japan sided with the majority. Had all the Latin American states and the Soviet Union participated in the vote, there probably would have been a majority against the "international standard." Because of the almost even split, the Conference adjourned without formulating any draft convention on the responsibility of states.

The norm of "prompt, adequate and effective" compensation has been further weakened since World War II by expropriations without payment of what was considered adequate compensation in countries of Eastern Europe, in Iran, Egypt, Cuba, and elsewhere. Attempts of the capital-exporting states to write the requirement of compensation into a widely accepted multilateral agreement have not been successful. The Asian African Legal Consultative Committee,[111] with Japan as the lone dissenter, has rejected the principle of an "international standard" of treatment of aliens, and

[110] G. H. Hackworth, "Responsibility of States for Damages Caused in Their Territory to the Person or Property of Foreigners," *AJIL*, Vol. 24, No. 3 (July 1930), p. 500. Cuba and Latvia abstained.

[111] The Committee was set up in November 1956 by Burma, Ceylon, India, Indonesia, Iraq, Japan, and Syria as the Asian Legal Consultative Committee. It was enlarged to include Morocco, Pakistan, Sudan, and the United Arab Republic. The word "African" was added to the title in 1958. The members are not regarded as official government representatives. See *Reports* of the Second (1958), Third (1960), and Fourth (1961) Sessions of the Committee, published by the Secretariat of the Committee in New Delhi; also, Kenzo Takayanagi and Hideo Tanaka, "The First Session of the Asian Legal Consultative Committee," *The Japanese Annual of International Law*, No. 2 (1958), p. 110.

[112] Asian African Legal Consultative Committee, *Reports*, 3rd Sess., 1960, pp. 83ff; 4th Sess., 1961, pp. 43, 46, 49, 141-142.

has drafted a convention that provides for payment for expropriated foreign property "in accordance with local laws, regulations and orders."[112]

The view that the "international standard" of treatment of aliens, or at least the requirement of "prompt, adequate and effective" compensation, is not or should not be a generally binding norm of international law, has also been expressed by some jurists from the less developed nations in the International Law Commission and in the literature.[113] It is probable that if the formula were squarely put to a vote in the General Assembly, it would be rejected by a majority composed of most of the less developed nations and the Soviet bloc. It can no longer be counted on to protect the interests of foreign investors in all the less developed countries. In this matter, the attainment of independence by so many capital-importing nations has certainly contributed to the weakening of a norm of international law which once seemed firmly established.

It has been sometimes pointed out that the legal content of the "international standard" of treatment of aliens, as it was traditionally understood and enforced, coincided in large part with what are regarded today as basic human rights. But the less developed nations, smarting under a sense of powerlessness and inferiority, regarded this institution as an imposition by the more powerful states. The resentment was intensified by the coercive measures—including military force—that the more advanced powers sometimes employed, not only to enforce their interpretation of the "standard," but also to exact concessions and other special privileges for their nationals and to intervene in the domestic affairs of the weaker states. In the strong words of a Mexican diplomat,

[113] See, for example, *Yearbook of the International Law Commission, 1957* (New York, United Nations, 1958) Vol. 1, pp. 155, 159-160; *ibid., 1959,* Vol. 1, p. 151; *ibid., 1960,* Vol. 1, p. 264; J. Castañeda, "The Underdeveloped Nations and the Development of International Law," *International Organization,* Vol. 15, No. 1 (Winter 1961), p. 38; S. N. Guha Roy, "Is the Law of Responsibility of States for Injuries to Aliens a Part of Universal International Law?", *AJIL,* Vol. 55, No. 4 (Oct. 1961), p. 863. Similar views have been voiced in the Sixth Committee.

"the doctrine of responsibility of states was merely the legal garb that served to cloak and protect the imperialistic interests of the international oligarchy during the nineteenth century and the first part of the twentieth."[114]

Attitudes and Motivations

The understandable resentment that debtor nations feel against a rule of law established and enforced by their creditors has been only one of the factors that have weakened the force of international legal norms designed to protect foreign business interests. Another is the world-wide trend toward state intervention in economic life, manifested in an extreme form in the Communist countries, but evident also in the Western and less developed nations.

When states such as the United Kingdom and France nationalize industry, as they did after World War II, they generally have the means to assure payment of compensation acceptable to the private owners, including any foreign investors. The less developed countries, however, are often unable to pay on terms approximating the "prompt, adequate and effective" compensation formula. When there is strong domestic pressure for social reform, it is likely to take precedence over the interests of foreign investors. There is also a widespread fear that foreigners are depleting irreplaceable natural resources and that the nation is not getting a proper share of the proceeds of the exploitation.

Another factor of particular importance in newly independent nations, but not wholly confined to them, is that many foreign investments were made during the colonial period when the nation could not express its will. They are now felt to be a vestige of the colonial "bondage" that must be wiped out if the nation is to be really free to enjoy its resources. This factor may also be of importance in countries which, though formally "independent," were under strong foreign influence which they were too weak to resist. It prob-

[114] Castañeda, *op. cit.*, p. 39.

ably contributed to the Communist seizure of power in China and is likely to play a significant role in the future policies of many countries not yet independent.

On the issue of protection of foreign investments, as on some others, the tendency of the less developed nations to challenge traditional international law has the encouragement of the Soviet bloc, although the motivation is not the same. The Communists are interested in weakening the economic and political power of the West and in undermining the private enterprise system throughout the world. The less developed nations are interested primarily in asserting their sovereignty and freedom in pursuing social reform and in getting the full benefit of their resources.

An important factor contributing to the decline of the effectiveness of the traditional norms protecting foreign investments has been the growing reluctance of the capital-exporting states to enforce their claims by coercive means. Although the cold war and the fear that the use of coercion would play into the hands of the Communists have served to strengthen this reluctance, its origins may be traced back to the inter-war period. It is related to the revulsion against war, the mounting costs of coercion, and the wide acceptance of the view that as an instrument of policy the use of force by one state against another is no longer lawful.

It must be emphasized that we are speaking not of hard and fast policies pursued by the less developed nations as if they formed a solid bloc, but of tendencies. Had they formed a monolithic and determined bloc, the less developed nations, with Soviet support, could have pushed through the General Assembly—where the capital exporting countries from a small minority—a resolution unequivocally declaring that there is no duty under international law to pay compensation for expropriated foreign property. Even though not formally binding, such a resolution would weaken the legal position of the capital-exporting states. In fact, the more extreme proposals, sponsored largely by Soviet-bloc states, have generally failed to get enough support from the less developed nations to be adopted. Thus, a Soviet amendment to the 1962 resolution on natural wealth and resources[115] which would have confirmed "the inalienable right of peoples and nations to the unobstructed execution of nationalization, expropriation and other measures," was rejected by 48 votes to 34, with 21 abstentions. Among the negative votes were those of ten African and Asian states (significantly including India) and sixteen Latin American nations (including Mexico and Brazil). Nineteen African and Asian and two Latin American states abstained. Only twenty-three African and Asian states—less than half the total number in the United Nations—cast their votes for this Soviet proposal.[116] Another Soviet amendment that would have "unreservedly" supported "measures taken by peoples and States to re-establish or strengthen their sovereignty over natural wealth and resources" and considered "inadmissible acts aimed at obstructing the creation, defence and strengthening of that sovereignty" had a larger measure of support. It was adopted in the Second Committee, but rejected in the plenary meeting by 41 votes to 38, with 15 abstentions. In the latter vote, it was supported by twenty-six African and Asian and two Latin American states. Again, the Soviets succeeded in attracting the votes of fewer than half of the African and Asian members of the United Nations.[117] Many of the spokesmen for the less developed nations in the course of the debate sought to reassure capital-exporting states by pointing to the clause on compensation and denying any intention to promote confiscation of foreign investments.[118]

---

[115] General Assembly Res. 1803 (XVII), 14 Dec. 1962.

[116] United Nations Doc. A/PV. 1193, 14 Dec. 1962, pp. 71-76.

[117] United Nations Docs. A/5344/Add. 1, 12 Dec. 1962, and A/PV.1194, 14 Dec. 1962, pp. 2-5.

[118] For the debates, see United Nations Docs. A/C.2/SRs. 834, 841-842, 845-846, 848, 850-859, 12 Nov.—7 Dec. 1962, and A/PVs. 1193-1194, 14 Dec. 1962. See, further, K. N. Gess, "Permanent Sovereignty Over Natural Resources: An Analytical Review of the United Nations Declaration and Its Genesis," *International and Comparative Law Quarterly*, Vol. 13, Part 2 (April 1964), p. 398; and Association of the Bar of the City of New York, Report of the Committee on International Law, *The Record*, Vol. 18, No. 6 (June 1963), p. 377.

The fear of offending states that extend economic and other assistance—as was frankly admitted in the debates— and the desire to obtain the largest possible majorities affirming permanent sovereignty over natural resources were largely responsible for this attitude rather than solicitude for the existing norms of international law. It suggests, however, an absence of doctrinaire and uncompromising hostility to the interests of the capital-exporting nations. Further, it suggests a recognition of the important role foreign private capital can play in economic development. Some of the spokesmen for the less developed countries seem to admit that there is a duty under international law to pay compensation for expropriated foreign property.[119] A further indication of the reluctance of the capital-importing states officially to repudiate this duty may be seen in the fact that acts of expropriation, such as those in Iran, Egypt, and Cuba, have been usually accompanied by provisions for compensation, although on terms not regarded as satisfactory by the investors.

Despite this pragmatic recognition of a common interest, many of the less developed nations have been reluctant to enter into general treaty commitments—even of a bilateral nature—not to expropriate foreign investments without the payment of just compensation. The United States, which is the prime source of private investment capital, has been able to conclude treaties containing such commitments with only eight less developed nations—the Republic of China (Taiwan), Ethiopia, Korea, Muscat, Nicaragua, Pakistan, and Vietnam—since World War II.[120] Many of these are heavily dependent on the United States for military and political support and cannot be regarded as representative

---

[119] See, for example, the remarks of Prime Minister Mossadegh of Iran, made at the height of the Anglo-Iranian oil crisis, SCOR, 6th Year, 563rd Mtg., 17 Oct. 1951, para. 125; and of the representative of Ceylon, United Nations Doc. A/C.2/SR.853, 30 Nov. 1962, p. 7.

[120] Yet provisions for the protection of foreign property against expropriation without just compensation appear, curiously enough, in some bilateral treaties between less developed nations. See, for example, Art. 3 of the 1950 Treaty of Commerce between Afghanistan and India. *United Nations Treaty Series.* Vol. 167, p. 112. Property protection clauses also appear in recent treaties of European states and Japan with some less developed nations.

of the attitudes of the less developed nations as a group. Even these treaties, furthermore, do not provide full security for the investors, if only because they are terminable on notice. Schemes for general multilateral conventions guaranteeing foreign investments against confiscation are highly unlikely to attract the support of a significant number of less developed countries. The newly independent nations, in particular, would be loath in many cases to limit their freedom of action with respect to property acquired by foreigners during the colonial period. But unwillingness to enter into treaty commitments of a general nature does not preclude agreements to guarantee specific new investments on a selective basis.

Furthermore, experience indicates that the interest of the less developed nations in the maintenance of normal relations with the capital-exporting states and their business enterprises often leads to the settlement of foreign claims for expropriated investments and prematurely terminated concessions. Even the Communist governments of eastern Europe have entered into agreements with most of the capital-exporting states for the payment of lump-sum compensation on an installment basis for expropriations effected after World War II.[121] Mexico and Iran reached agreements with the oil companies whose investments they nationalized, and Egypt settled the claim that arose from the premature cancellation of the Suez Canal concession. The compensation obtained by foreign investors pursuant to such settlements is generally not regarded in Western financial and legal circles as fully adequate. Nevertheless, it serves to alleviate the practical effects of the tendency of the less developed nations to disregard or challenge the traditional norms of international law designed for the protection of foreign property and business interests.

The solution of the problems posed by actual or possible

---

[121] White, *loc. cit.*

nationalization of foreign investments is likely to proceed along two lines. First, there is a tendency in the West to recognize that the formula of "prompt, adequate and effective" compensation may be unrealistic in many situations and that it may have to give way to the more flexible test of "reasonableness." The reasonableness of compensation would be determined in the light of many relevant factors other than the full value of the property.[122] In many negotiated settlements, such a test has in fact already been applied. Second, future investments can be protected by specific arrangements and guarantees, including insurance of the investment by the investor's state, which in case of expropriation would become subrogated to his claims. Programs of such insurance or guarantees are already in operation in the United States and some other capital-exporting nations.[123]

Width of the Territorial Sea

The attitudes of the less developed nations diverge from those of the West at other points. With regard to the law of the sea, for example, most of these nations have thrown the weight of their numbers against the traditional three-mile doctrine of the width of the territorial sea that is still upheld by the leading maritime powers of the West and by Japan. Some of them have also tended to expand the maritime area under their control in other ways. In the cases of Indonesia and the Philippines, this has been done by claiming all of the waters between the islands that constitute the territory of these states. The leading maritime nations of the West and Japan regard the extension of the width of the territorial sea as a threat to their interests. They have also refused to

---

[122] See, e.g., F. G. Dawson and B. H. Weston, " 'Prompt, Adequate and Effective': A Universal Standard of Compensation?" *Fordham Law Review*, Vol. 30, No. 4 (April 1962), p. 727; Friedmann, *op. cit.*, pp. 206-210; A. A. Fatouros, "International Law and the Third World," *Virginia Law Review*, Vol. 50, No. 5 (June 1964), pp. 799-817.

[123] See S. D. Metzger, "Property in International Law," *Virginia Law Review*, Vol. 50, No. 4 (May 1964), p. 594.

recognize the claims to all the water between the islands of large archipelagoes.

The challenge to the traditional limit of the territorial sea is by no means confined to the newly independent nations. Mexico and Iceland were among the more determined opponents of the three-mile rule at the 1958 and 1960 Geneva Conferences on the Law of the Sea. Many Latin American countries claim more than the traditional three miles as territorial waters. Some, notably Chile, Ecuador, and Peru, have asserted control over as much as 200 miles. The governments of the Sino-Soviet bloc, with the notable exception of Poland, generally claim a width of twelve miles. At the 1958 and 1960 Geneva Conferences, the coalition of most of the less developed nations, old and new, with the Soviet bloc and such states as Iceland made hopeless the prospects for the reaffirmation of the three-mile rule.

These nations are motivated by a number of factors. Perhaps the most important, particularly among the Latin American and such countries as Iceland, is the desire to protect the fisheries off their coasts against overfishing by foreign fishermen employing modern and efficient equipment. Even where there is no immediate danger of depletion, some of the less developed nations fear that, because of lack of capital and enterprise, their own fishermen would be unable to compete with better equipped foreigners.

Considerations of security have been another factor. In case of armed conflict between the West and the Soviet bloc, the neutralist nations would like to keep hostilities away from their coastlines. Even in time of peace, many of the weaker nations would like to lessen the opportunities for pressure by naval demonstrations, for example. The naval powers of the West, and particularly the United States, by the same token, want the greatest possible freedom for the deployment of their sea power.[124] The Arab states have a

124 See C. M. Franklin, *The Law of the Sea: Some Recent Developments*, U.S. Naval War College, *International Law Studies*, Vol. 53 (1959-1960) (Washington, GPO, 1961), pp. 116-123.

special interest in a wide territorial sea as a means of establishing exclusive control of the Gulf of Aqaba and denying its use to Israel. In the attitude of the Soviet bloc, considerations of military advantage and protection of fisheries both play a part.[125] In addition, there may be a psychological drive in the weaker states, particularly the newly independent nations, and even among the Communist ruling elites to assert themselves by claiming sovereignty over as large an area as possible.

As in the matter of the "international standard," the less developed nations by no means form a solid and determined bloc on the issue of the width of the territorial sea. This was evident at the 1960 Geneva Conference in the crucial vote on a United States-Canadian compromise proposal to extend the territorial sea to six miles, with a further six-mile zone in which the coastal states would have exclusive control of fisheries after a ten-year period. Fifteen African and Asian and thirteen Latin American nations cast affirmative votes, while eleven African and Asian and six Latin American states were opposed. The proposal fell only one vote short of the two-thirds required for adoption.[126] It was strenuously opposed by the Soviet bloc.

The desire of the governments of some of the less developed nations to extend their territorial waters is tempered by the realization that sovereignty implies responsibility as well as authority, and that the smaller and poorer nations may find it difficult to police large expanses of the sea adequately. Moreover, a total of twelve miles of exclusive fishing rights—without sovereignty for all purposes—would satisfy many of the states opposed to the traditional three-mile limit.

A lack of agreement within the international community

125 A Soviet jurist in a recent book advocates the adoption of the principle that the high seas should be used only for "peaceful" purposes and that naval warfare and even peacetime naval maneuvers on the high seas should be outlawed. S. V. Molodtsov, *Mezhdunarodno-Pravovoi Rezhim Otkrytogo Moria i Kontinental'nogo Shelfa* (Moscow, Izdatel'stvo Ikademii Nauk SSSR, 1960), pp. 107-136.

126 United Nations Doc. A/CONF. 19/8, 13th Plenary Mtg., 26 Apr. 1960, para. 18; see also A. H. Dean, "The Second Geneva Conference on the Law of the Sea: The Fight for Freedom of the Seas," *AJIL*, Vol. 54, No. 4 (Oct. 1960), p. 751.

on the proper width of the territorial sea is certain to produce friction for some time to come. By itself, however, it is no cause for alarm. A gradual adjustment of conflicting interests is likely to take place and, indeed, has already begun with the conclusion of bilateral agreements on fishing rights, such as those between the United Kingdom on the one hand and Denmark, Iceland, and Norway on the other.[127] It can be furthered by the conclusion of multilateral treaties for more effective conservation of certain stocks of fish, and by assistance to less developed nations in the modernization of their fishing industries to enable them to compete more effectively. The 1960 Conference on the Law of the Sea adopted a resolution favoring such assistance.[128]

The problem of disagreement on the width of the territorial sea is likely to be alleviated if not completely solved by the growing acceptance of the idea that it is permissible to establish fishery control zones beyond the limits of the territorial sea. A number of Western nations, including the United Kingdom and Canada as well as Norway, Iceland, and Denmark, have already established such zones, which are now expressly authorized by the new European Fisheries Convention.[129]

General acceptance of fishery control zones would permit many states to protect their fishing interests adequately without extending their territorial sea. But while the controversy over the width of the territorial sea continues, we are witnessing, in fact, the appearance of several norms operating within particular groups of states. As between two states claiming a twelve-mile zone, for example, that width amounts to a norm of international law; as between two states still insisting on the three-mile rule, the rule still prevails. In effect,

---

[127] See D. H. N. Johnson, "Developments since the Geneva Conference of 1958 and 1960: Anglo-Scandinavian Agreements Concerning the Territorial Sea and Fishing Limits," *International and Comparative Law Quarterly*, Vol. 10, Part 3 (July 1961), p. 587.

[128] *Second United Nations Conference on the Law of the Sea*, 1960, Official Records, Sales No. 60.V.6 (New York, United Nations), Final Act, Annex, p. 176.

[129] For text, see *AJIL*, Vol. 58, No. 4 (Oct. 1964), p. 1070.

we have several norms of particular international law instead of a single norm of general international law.

The "international standard" and the three-mile limit, as norms of international law, have certain characteristics in common. Both have been developed and, until recently, were enforced by the stronger, more advanced Western powers and Japan. Neither was ever accepted wholeheartedly by the entire international community. Both norms have been weakened by the independence of the former colonial areas and, in part, by the new reluctance of the stronger states to use coercive means of enforcement.

Other Issues

In the law of treaties, the less developed nations, like the Soviet bloc, have tended to oppose the "unanimity doctrine" of the admissibility and effect of reservations to multilateral conventions. This is the view that a state cannot become a party to a treaty with a reservation to which any of the parties objects. These same nations have tended to show preference for the so-called Pan-American Rule (under which the reserving state becomes a party to the treaty with respect to other parties that do not object to the reservation). The United States has also tended to support the Pan American Rule, which is clearly gaining ground, and the division of opinion on this matter has had no serious effect on the international community.[130]

An area of international law that is clearly of special interest to the newly independent nations is that of state succession, which is currently under study by the International Law Commission. In this area, there are few agreed "traditional" norms. Some newly independent nations have voluntarily

130 See Bishop, *op. cit.;* W. W. Cox, "Reservations to Multipartite Conventions," *Proceedings of the American Society of International Law* (1952), p. 26; O. Schachter, "The Question of Treaty Reservations at the 1959 General Assembly," *AJIL.,* Vol. 54, No. 2 (Apr. 1960), p. 372; *Report of the International Law Commission,* GAOR: 17th Sess., 1962, Suppl. No. 9 (A/5209), pp. 18-25. A more serious problem may be presented by the doctrine of "unequal" treaties. See p. 93.

agreed to the inclusion of "devolution clauses" in agreements with their former metropoles. These clauses provide that the new states take over the rights and duties applicable to them as dependent territories under treaties made by their predecessors. Many new states have also voluntarily declared themselves bound by various multilateral treaties to which their predecessors were parties.[131]

There is, however, a strong tendency among newly independent states to question the duty to respect property rights and concessions acquired by foreigners during the colonial period. Although under traditional international law, pre-acquired property rights were not disturbed by a transfer of sovereignty, some of these states asked the General Assembly to declare that "the obligations of international law cannot apply to alleged rights acquired before the accession to full national sovereignty of formerly colonized countries."[132] The 1962 Assembly resolution on permanent sovereignty over natural resources specifically states that nothing in its paragraph on nationalization, expropriation, and compensation "in any way prejudices the position of any Member State" on any aspect of the question of the rights and obligations of successor states and governments in respect of property acquired before independence.

On the issue of sovereign immunity, a majority of the Asian African Legal Consultative Committee has favored the "restrictive" doctrine (i.e., the view that a state is not entitled to immunity from suit in the courts of another state with respect to claims arising out of its commercial activities). This view is gaining increasing support in western Europe and the Unted States. In the Committee, only Indonesia

---

[131] See D. P. O'Connell, "Independence and Succession to Treaties," *British Year Book of International Law, 1962,* p. 84.

[132] See, especially, the remarks of the Algerian delegate, United Nations Doc. A/C.2/SR.851, 28 Nov. 1962, p. 6.

[133] Asian African Legal Consultative Committee, Third Sess., 1960, *Report,* pp. 55, 57, 63-69. A Thai jurist has written a valuable monograph upholding the "restrictive" doctrine. See Sompong Sucharitkul, *State Immunities and Trading Activities in International Law* (New York, Praeger, 1959).

expressed decided preference for the "absolute" immunity doctrine that is strongly upheld by the Soviet Union.[133]

At the 1958 Geneva Conference on the Law of the Sea, a Soviet-bloc attempt to write into the Convention on the Territorial Sea and the Contiguous Zone a reference to the alleged immunity of government-operated trading vessels from the civil jurisdiction of the coastal state in the territorial sea mustered only ten affirmative votes (presumably those of the Soviet bloc and Yugoslavia) and was decisively defeated.[134]

In most other areas of international law, the attitude of the less developed nations toward norms accepted in the West has not been sufficiently distinctive to present any real problems. Minor variations in points of view among the different states are, of course, frequently manifested but such variations have not been serious enough to merit discussion here. The assertion that the newly independent nations are not bound by old norms in the making of which they had no part thus does not imply a wholesale rejection of the contents of traditional international law; rather it must be regarded as an expression of the resentment the newly independent nations still feel over their colonial past and as an assertion of their sovereignty and equality. It also serves as a reminder to the older states that the views of the newcomers are not to be disregarded in the formulation and further development of the law of nations. Nevertheless, such an assertion suggests a departure from the important principle of international order, long accepted, that, on being admitted into the international community, a new state is automatically bound by all the pre-existing norms of general international law. In the older and previously dominant part of the international community, it cannot but cause a disquieting sense of uncertainty and instability.

Consternation has also been caused in Western legal and political circles by the tendency of some less developed coun-

---

[134] *United Nations Conference on the Law of the Sea, Official Records*, Vol. III, Sales No. 58.V.4 (New York, United Nations), 1st Cmtte., 43rd Mtg., 11 Apr. 1958, p. 132, para. 1.

tries to change or challenge the *status quo,* even by forcible means, to the detriment of certain Western states and with little regard for international legal norms. The seizure of Goa by India in 1961 is the most obvious example of this tendency. At the seventeenth General Assembly session, Panama attacked the treaty by which the United States obtained control of the Canal Zone, and Venezuela demanded a revision of its boundary with British Guiana, which had been determined by arbitration in 1899. Political conflicts with more advanced states have been the occasion for the seizure of the property of the nationals of these powers, such as Dutch property in Indonesia and United States property in Cuba, on the pretext of reprisals, in disregard not only of the "international standard," but also of the "equality of treatment" standard favored by many less developed countries. Support openly given by many new nations to revolts against colonial rule in countries such as Algeria and Angola is inconsistent with the doctrines of sovereignty and non-intervention, but is sought to be justified by the principles of self-determination and anti-colonialism. Some new nations, moreover, do not fully observe legal restraints on the use of force and intervention even in their mutual relations.

There is resentment among Asians, Africans, and some Latin Americans, against what appears to them a double standard—reliance by the more advanced states on the binding nature of arrangements obtained during the colonial era by force or pressure and, at the same time, their denial today of the lawfulness of the use of force by less developed nations to uproot these fruits of past aggressions. Even today, as they are quick to point out, the behavior of major Western powers, as in the invasion of Suez in 1956 or of Cuba in 1961, is not always lawful. India sought to justify its seizure of Goa by characterizing the Portuguese rule there as "perpetual aggression."[135]

---

[135] See J. S. Bains, *India's International Disputes* (New York, Asia Publishing House, 1962), p. 197.

In the attempt to provide legal justification for their efforts to change the *status quo,* the less developed nations increasingly rely on the argument that "unequal" or "inequitable" treaties, and treaties imposed by duress, are invalid *ab initio.* Attacking the treaty by which the United States obtained the Canal Zone, for example, the foreign minister of Panama called it "humiliating, injurious, unjust and inequitable," and said that it "does not conform to the principles, precepts and norms of international law, justice and international morality universally accepted today."[136]

The record does not fully bear out the assertion that the less developed nations, particularly the newly independent countries of Asia and Africa, are unwilling to resort to judicial settlement or arbitration of international controversies. Of the four contentious proceedings pending before the International Court of Justice at the end of 1962, for example, three had been initiated by African states—two by Ethiopia and Liberia against South Africa, and one by Cameroon against the United Kingdom. Previously, the Court had decided disputes between Colombia and Peru, Honduras and Nicaragua, and Cambodia and Thailand.[137] Many of the less developed nations supported the decision of the sixteenth General Assembly to ask the International Court for an advisory opinion on the applicability of Article 17 (2) of the Charter to the expenses incurred in the United Nations operations in the Middle East and the Congo. These states, however, have shown even less enthusiasm for the compulsory jurisdition of the Court than have Western nations. At the end of 1964, only ten African and Asian nations were among the forty states that had accepted it under the optional clause of Article 36 of the Court's Statute. This may stem from fear that the Court might apply the norms of international law that the less developed nations tend to reject, or might uphold the legal rights of the Western nations against attempts

---

[136] *The New York Times,* 26 Sept. 1962.

[137] It may be noted that in the inter-war period some Latin American nations avoided submitting to arbitration claims arising out of expropriation measures.

to change the *status quo* inherited from the colonial era. There have been, moreover, very few Asian and African judges on the Court. This may be a factor in the cautious attitude of many newly independent states toward the Court. But these considerations alone hardly suffice to explain why many less developed nations oppose clauses in new multilateral conventions that would enable any of the parties to submit disputes arising under the conventions to the Court.

Impact of Cultural Traditions

Does the non-Western cultural background of the Asian and African states tend to make them adopt attitudes toward international law different from those of the Western nations? Some Western and non-Western writers have suggested that, in Asia at least, the basic cultural tradition is to favor mediation and conciliation rather than the strict application of law as a means of settling disputes, and to regard law as a set of broad and flexible principles permitting of adjustment and compromise rather than as a body of rigid technical rules.[138] But generalizations about "Asia" or "Africa" are dangerous, for they tend to overlook the large variety of cultures and traditions that exist within those continents.

So far as attitudes toward specific norms of international law are concerned, all the evidence points to the conclusion that present interest, rightly or wrongly understood, rather than cultural tradition has been the immediately decisive factor.[139] Differences in the levels of economic and political development lie behind the more extreme differences be-

[138] See, for example, R. P. Anand, "Rôle of the 'New' Asian-African Countries in the Present International Legal Order," *AJIL,* Vol. 56, No. 2 (Apr. 1962), pp. 383, 394-395; Syatauw, *op. cit.,* pp. 22-23. There is a division of opinion among Asian jurists on this point. *Cf.,* for example, Anand, *op. cit.,* with Syatauw, *op. cit.,* pp. 22-27; see also R. P. Anand, "Attitude of the 'New' Asian-African Countries Toward the International Court of Justice," *International Studies* (New Delhi), Vol. 4, No. 1 (July 1962), p. 119.

[139] Nations of widely different cultural backgrounds have, for example, been united in opposition to the traditional norms on expropriation of foreign property and the width of the territorial sea.

tween legal institutions. Much of Western law, including international law, has developed in response to the requirements of the Western business civilization. As non-Western countries have moved toward fuller participation in present-day economic and political life, they have come to realize that many of their legal traditions are no longer adequate to their needs. Most of these countries are adopting, in varying degrees, modern institutions, largely derived from those of the West. In some, reception of Western law has already reached an advanced stage. In the West itself law does not stand still. The effects on law of greater state participation in economic life and the rise of the "welfare state" are likely to be worldwide. In the long run, this factor should serve to reduce differences in attitudes toward international law.

Cultural factors, however, may influence a nation's attitude toward international law in various ways. They may have a role in determining the level of a country's development and thus, indirectly, its specific interests with respect to particular norms of international law. They may enter into the very definition of "the national interest." A nation's attitude toward the role of law in world affairs may reflect, however subtly, the role that domestic law plays in the life of the nation and the extent to which international law is known and understood within its ruling elite.

Among the less developed nations, there are wide differences. In some of the newly independent countries where an educated elite has just begun to form, there is a critical shortage of all kinds of specialists, including persons trained in international law. In others there are a substantial number of lawyers, civil servants, and university professors who are in varying degrees familiar with international law. These countries are contributing significantly to the literature of international law. All of the newly independent nations, however, suffer in varying degrees not only from a lack of material resources such as libraries, but also from the fact that under the colonial regime their elites were given few, if any, opportunities to participate actively in the handling of foreign affairs, and had little reason, therefore, to acquire a knowledge of international law. At the seventeenth General Assembly in 1962, many of the less developed nations acknowledged the importance of removing deficiencies in international law training; they strongly supported a resolution requesting the Secretary-General to study and report on the possibilities of technical assistance to promote the teaching, study, dissemination, and wider appreciation of international law.[140]

It is tempting to ascribe to non-Western cultural factors the attraction international legal slogans of great generality seem to have for a number of the less developed countries, particularly for the newly independent nations. In the absence of definitive comparative studies of traditional attitudes toward law in various parts of the world, the possibility of such a relationship can be neither categorically denied nor affirmed. But those who emphasize the effect of cultural heritage on attitudes toward international law tend to overlook the diversity of approaches to law that exist in the West as well as in the non-Western parts of the world. The recent trend in the West, particularly in the United States, is toward a less technical view of the law. The increasingly influential school of international law created by Myres S. McDougal of Yale University regards law as a process of decision into which all relevant factors, and not merely technical norms, enter. It virtually identifies law with policy and calls the study of law "a policy science."[141] While this position is not yet widely accepted in the West, it points up the danger of wholly

140 General Assembly Res. 1816 (XVII), 18 Dec. 1962. On the basis of a report submitted by the Secretary-General in 1963, the General Assembly established a Special Committee to prepare a plan and submit it to the Assembly at its nineteenth session. General Assembly Res. 1968 (XVIII), 16 Dec. 1963. The Committee reported in 1965. United Nations Doc. A/5887, 17 Feb. 1965.

141 See McDougal et al., op. cit.; also, M. S. McDougal, "Interantional Law, Power and Policy: A Contemporary Conception," Recueil des Cours, Vol. 82 (1953-I), p. 137. For a full discussion of the role of cultural background in attitudes toward international law, see Friedmann, op. cit., pp. 297-324; but cf. Fatouros, op. cit., pp. 788-790.

identifying the West with a rigid, technical conception of law that neglects broad principles of justice and overlooks the necessity for adjustment and compromise.

Furthermore, the Western cultural tradition is no guarantee of adherence to "the rule of law" in either domestic or international affairs. Western commentators tend to forget all too easily that in the twentieth century one of the most arrogantly nihilistic challenges to the traditional principles of law and morality came from a highly developed and educated nation in the heart of Europe with an impeccably Western ethnic and cultural pedigree—Nazi Germany.

Pessimistic prophecies concerning the impact of cultural differences on the ability of the new nations to participate in a system of world public order side by side with the West may be dangerously self-fulfilling. Instead of constantly dwelling on these differences, those who would serve the cause of progress toward a better future should emphasize the common humanity of all peoples and the basic unity of mankind.

Some diversity in attitudes toward law is bound to remain in the non-Western world, as in the West. But as the process of reception of modern law continues, there should be less and less reason to fear that differences of cultural heritage have produced an unbridgeable gap between Western and non-Western attitudes toward law in general and international law in particular. The long-term trend is toward greater uniformity of legal systems and traditions.

Although the less developed nations tend to question some of the content of customary international law, they are showing awareness of the role of international law in modern life by signing treaties, becoming parties to multilateral conventions, and joining international organizations. Indeed, the Western commentators who speak of a "crisis" in international law seem to overlook the increasing role that treaties and organizations are playing in the process of international regulation of the conduct of states. Customary international law, it is true, provides the essential framework within which treaties operate and organizations function. In this sense, consensus manifested through "custom" may still be regarded as the primary source of international law. But the norms regulating the conduct of states that are laid down in multilateral and bilateral treaties, or prescribed by international organs acting within the scope of powers conferred upon them by treaties, are today far greater in number and, in the main, more specific than those found in customary international law. Since treaties generally bind only those states parties to them, treaty law is not "universal"; it is, nevertheless, of steadily growing importance in the life of nations.

The less developed nations, including the newly independent states, have become parties to multilateral treaties, such as the Universal Postal Convention and the International Civil Aviation Convention, for their obvious practical advantages. Their adhesion to treaties that prescribe social and humanitarian standards for primarily domestic application may be motivated by prestige considerations and may be less indicative of willingness to become really bound by international regulation. But non-compliance with treaties of the former kind is likely to be quickly noted and to bring protests from the other parties. Yet the newly independent states become parties in large numbers to this kind of treaty.

Particularly significant is the willingness of many less developed nations to participate in organizations and treaties, such as the International Monetary Fund (IMF) and the General Agreement on Tariffs and Trade (GATT), which involve some regulation of international economic relations. Among the members of IMF are most of the leading countries of Asia and Africa and all the Latin American states. A considerable number of newly independent nations have become parties to GATT. Eighteen African states have become associated with the European Economic Community. Considerations of sovereignty thus do not prevent the less developed nations from entering into complex economic and financial arrangements that limit their freedom of action when such arrangements offer significant advantages. The readiness of the newly independent nations to join international organizations is due at least in part to the desire to benefit from technical assistance and other aid programs.

A Western jurist has drawn a strikingly imaginative parallel between the emergence of less developed nations into a position of greater political influence and the rise of the working classes to power in the West. In both cases, there has been a process of democratization of the legal community. The previously submerged classes have demanded fuller participation in the law-making process and revision of the legal systems developed by the older ruling classes. They have also pressed for welfare legislation. At times, the spokesmen for the emergent classes have seemed uncouth and dangerously radical. In the Western democracies, the result has been a compromise. The continuity of the legal system has not been destroyed; much of the old law has remained. Nor have the old ruling classes been completely dispossessed, although they have lost most of the exclusive privilege they once enjoyed. There has emerged the modern democratic "welfare" state in which the previously submerged classes have obtained substantially what they wanted. It was only when the old ruling classes stubbornly refused to heed the demands of the masses or were too slow in adjusting to them that violent upheavals swept away the old order completely.[142]

The "welfare" interest of the less developed nations has been expressed in several ways, but can be summarized in two basic demands: more aid for development, and better terms of trade. Indeed, it has been suggested that the basic malaise of the less developed nations about international law stems from the failure of the latter to support their demand for greater aid from the richer states in the modernization process.[143] In effect, they want the power to tax the rich. In

142 B. V. A. Röling, *International Law in an Expanded World* (Amsterdam, Djambatan, 1960), pp. 56-86.
143 See R. A. Falk, "Appendix to Report of Committee on Peaceful Coexistence: The New States and International Law," in *Proceedings and Committee Reports of the American Branch of the International Law Association, 1963-1964*, p. 93.

many international organizations, they press for higher budgets for technical assistance and the like, while the West and the U.S.S.R. often find themselves united in opposition to such budgets. The less developed nations are thus likely to favor conferring greater legislative powers on international organizations. But they are quite aware of the fact that their numerical strength is offset by the greater material power—economic, technological, and military—of the highly industrialized states. The prospect is for an extended period of gradual accommodation.

In the field of trade, the less developed countries as producers of primary commodities (food, fuel, raw materials) find themselves at a disadvantage vis-à-vis the highly industrialized nations. Furthermore, the latter sometimes impose quotas and other special restrictions on the imports of the products of the new manufacturing industries of the developing countries. The discontent of the latter with this situation brought about the convocation of the United Nations Conference on Trade and Development in Geneva in 1964. There, the less developed countries pressed for commodity agreements to assure adequate prices for their primary commodities, preferential treatment for their exports on a nonreciprocal basis, and an increase in the financial resources made available for their development. Despite much controversy, both the less developed countries and the highly industrialized nations of the West displayed a spirit of compromise and conciliation, leading some observers to appraise the results with cautious optimism. The Conference recommended the establishment of permanent organs to continue and develop the work of the United Nations in the field of trade

[144] "United Nations Conference on Trade and Development Adopts Final Act," U.S. Department of State *Bulletin,* Vol. 51, No. 1310 (3 Aug. 1964), p. 150; "The Significance of the United Nations Conference on Trade and Development," United Nations Doc. E/CONF.46/140, 9 July 1964. *Proceedings of the United Nations Conference on Trade and Development,* Vol. I, *Final Act and Report,* Sales No. 64.II.B. 11 (New York, United Nations, 1964); "Issues Before the Nineteenth General Assembly," *International Conciliation,* No. 550 (Nov. 1964), pp. 128-169; R. N. Gardner, *In Pursuit of World Order* (New York, Praeger, 1964), pp. 159-172; General Assembly Res. 1995 (XIX), 30 Dec. 1964.

and development. This recommendation has been accepted by the General Assembly.[144]

It has been suggested that the emergence of "the third world" with its distinctive demands has strengthened the stability of world public order by reducing bipolarity. The introduction of new elements of diversity, according to this view, has strengthened the role of international law and organization, since the need for cohesiveness is more evident in a pluralistic than in a bipolar world.[145]

[145] Fatouros, *op. cit.*, pp. 822-823.

95430

THE OUTLOOK

THE SENSE OF A "CRISIS" in international law experienced by many observers today is a product of the acceleration of the processes of change in the international community that is characteristic of our era. The factors that have caused this acceleration are well known. They include rapid technological progress; the rise of new ideologies and systems of public order, including militant communism; decolonization, itself spurred on by the Communist challenge to the West; the appearance of many new states of widely different cultural backgrounds and levels of development; rising demands for social reform; the fear of war and the growing reluctance of the more advanced states to protect their interests by coercive means; and the increase in the number and functions of international organizations. The processes of change have, on the one hand, tended to limit the operation or decrease the relevance of some traditional legal norms and, on the other hand, have created new areas of need for legal regulation. What then are the prospects for the future of international law in a divided, rapidly changing world?

At first glance, as has been seen, there appear to be many disturbing similarities between the attitudes of the Communist elites and those of the less developed nations, particularly the newly independent states, toward international law. Both the Communist elites and the less developed nations emphasize, for example, self-determination, anti-colonialism, equality, non-intervention, and invalidity of "unequal" treaties. The latter, like the Communist governments, tend to manipulate such highly general principles without much regard for consistency or reciprocity. Spokesmen for the newly independent nations, like those for the Soviet Union, tend to reject the traditional doctrine that norms of general international law are automatically binding on new states (and on states ruled by new governments) and claim freedom to decide by which of the old norms they will be bound. On the specific issues of "the international standard" and the three-mile width of the territorial sea, many of the less developed nations have ranged themselves with the Soviet bloc in opposing the traditional norms favored by the West and Japan. Many of the new nations, moreover, seem to espouse the Soviet-sponsored slogan of "peaceful coexistence," principally as a weapon in their struggle against "colonialism" in all its forms.[146]

Yet, on closer examination, the danger that the Communist elites and the less developed nations might form a coalition is seen to be illusory. The aims and motivations of most of the less developed countries diverge widely from those of the Communist elites. A large number of these nations have not supported Communist proposals on expropriation of foreign investments and the width of the territorial sea. Nor have they supported the Soviet bloc on the issue of sovereign immunity. The posture of these nations toward judicial settlement of international disputes, despite considerable reluctance to accept the compulsory jurisdiction of the International Court, is by no means identical with the basic Communist hostility to such settlement—as the submission of several cases to the Court by Latin American, African, and Asian states indicates. The Soviet Union has failed to gain the solid support of these countries for its position in the United Nations on many important political issues. Furthermore, the less developed nations have been far more willing than the Soviet bloc to participate in international regulatory organizations and arrangements such as ICAO, IMF, and GATT. And they failed to support the Soviets in sufficient strength to force the adoption by the

---

[146] See Hazard, "Coexistence, Co-operation, and the Common Law," *op. cit.*, pp. 23-24; and the Declaration adopted by the Conference of Heads of State or Government of Non-Aligned Countries, Cairo, Oct. 1964, in United Nations Doc. A/5763, 29 Oct. 1964, esp. pp. 14-16.

103

General Assembly of the slogan of "peaceful coexistence" and its Soviet interpretation. Instead, many of them joined the West in adopting the term "principles of international law concerning friendly relations and cooperation among states" to describe the "new international law" on the agenda of the Sixth Committee of the General Assembly.[147]

Some of the attitudes of the less developed nations, particularly those related to the real or fancied vestiges of colonialism, will continue to trouble the West for a long time to come. The relatively low level of economic development of most of the non-Western and Latin American states, and the continued dependence of these states on the industrial nations for capital and technical assistance, will tend to prolong feelings of inferiority and to breed suspicion that the more advanced nations are using their superior position to dominate the poorer countries. To minimize resentment, the colonial powers should not exact, at the time of the granting of independence or subsequently, agreements that the less developed states are likely to regard as burdensome, unfair, and inconsistent with their best interests. The West cannot —and does not—disregard either the distinctive viewpoints of the less developed nations, or their claim to full participation in the international law-making process. Experience indicates that even on the seemingly most intractable of issues—that of protection of foreign investments—adjustment, compromise, and settlement on mutually acceptable terms will continue to be possible, at least so long as nations do not choose the path of complete elimination of private enterprise from their economic life.

It would be a mistake to discount as mere verbiage the often expressed concern of the less developed nations for the strengthening and development of international law. Weak in material power, these nations must seek protection

[147] See Report of the Sixth Committee, United Nations Doc. A/5036, 15 Dec. 1961; and Paul Martin, "Co-existence or Friendly Relations? The Canadian Approach," in E. McWhinney, ed., *Law, Foreign Policy, and the East-West Détente, op. cit.,* p. 46.

and assistance in international law and organization. This does not mean, of course, that the less developed nations will have no distinctive points of view or will not attempt— as all nations have done—to use international law to promote their own real or fancied interests. Moreover, the less developed countries will insist on having their voices heard in the formulation and development of the law, and will utilize their collective numerical strength to maximize their influence in this process.

Customary international law has at times developed with considerable speed to provide for the regulation of new transnational needs and activities. The twentieth century has witnessed, for example, the rapid development of the doctrines of air sovereignty and the continental shelf. Nevertheless, the acceleration of the processes of change in the international community and the detailed nature of the regulation required for many new activities render custom an inadequate instrument for the formation of legal norms in response to all the new needs and expectations.

Recent trends in customary international law have been in the direction of expanding rather than contracting the sphere of territorial sovereignty or jurisdiction of states. This is evident, for example, in the extension of national sovereignty or control to airspace and the continental shelf, the greater use of "straight baselines" from which the territorial sea is measured, the establishment of fishery control zones beyond the territorial sea, and the adoption of the "restrictive" doctrine of sovereign immunity by many states.[148]

It would be a mistake to regard these trends as symptoms of a breakdown in world public order. The extension of national control over the continental shelf and the decline of "absolute" sovereign immunity serve to promote rather than weaken the rule of law. Had the continental shelf remained subject to the three-mile rule, there would have been less

---

148 The growth of the consensus that outer space and celestial bodies are not subject to national appropriation appears to be an exception.

105

"law and order" in it than there is today, and private investment in the exploitation of its riches would have been far more risky. In the absence of a regulatory treaty, the realistic alternative to national control was the traditional "freedom of the seas" with the attendant lack of detailed regulation and of safeguards for the investors' expectations. In this situation, therefore, the development of customary law has served to strengthen the rule of law by permitting states to substitute the specific norms and safeguards of their national legal systems for the vaguer standards of "the freedom of the seas." Similarly, the "restrictive" doctrine of sovereign immunity promotes the rule of law by permitting adjudication in national courts of many private claims against foreign states. But if specific regulation by truly international norms and procedures is needed, custom is too blunt an instrument. International norms and procedures of a high degree of specificity must be created by treaty.

The less developed nations may be expected to use their influence to strengthen the trend toward law-making by multilateral treaties, particularly on subjects of special interest to them. Nations with a close community of interest or with similar attitudes and institutions will continue, as in the past, to devise special norms to regulate their mutual relations. The network of multilateral and bilateral treaties will continue to increase in complexity. Regional legal institutions, such as those of Europe, will continue to be created by states with special common interests. The creation of such institutions and of other particular international law will strengthen rather than diminish the role of law in world affairs.[149]

The conclusion of treaties embracing limited numbers of states may seem to be a further impairment of the "universality" of international law. But such treaties continue to be made and to operate within the framework of the more basic and general rules that constitute "universal" international

---

[149] See Fatouros, *op. cit.*, pp. 818-823.

law. Among these general rules, those of the law of treaties—the rules concerning the conclusion, validity, interpretation, performance, revision, and termination of treaties—will continue to be of fundamental and perhaps increasing importance.

There will be sustained efforts to formulate and develop the basic customary rules in negotiated conventions similar to those on the law of the sea and on diplomatic relations.

Here, again, the fact that such conventions deal with general norms and yet are unlikely to be adhered to by all states —and thus formally to bind all states—might indicate a further breakdown in the universality of international law. Nevertheless, the necessities of international life will continue to demand a large measure of uniformity of basic rules, and many, if not all, of the rules formulated in the conventions may be expected to be universally accepted in practice.

The numerical strength of the less developed nations may also lead them to favor efforts to formulate and develop the law by declarations, adopted as resolutions by the General Assembly.[150] Such declarations are not formally binding. However, they have the appearance of expressing a world consensus and cannot be totally disregarded by national and international decision-makers. They may be employed to confirm and strengthen existing precedents and trends in international law, or to initiate new trends. General Assembly resolutions have already been so used.[151] Their use

---

[150] See Castañeda, *op. cit.*, pp. 44-48. In 1961, a Ceylonese delegate said that "multilateral treaties were the best source of international law, and all the United Nations resolutions could be regarded as such." GAOR: 16th Sess., 6th Cmtte., 716th Mtg., 20 Nov. 1961. In 1962, in the Sixth Committee, Iran, Iraq, Somalia, Cyprus, and India, as well as the Ukrainian SSR, spoke favorably of General Assembly declarations as a means of developing international law. The 1964 Soviet textbook accords to certain unanimously adopted resolutions of the General Assembly the role of sources of international law. Kozhevnikov, ed., *op. cit.* (1964), p. 43. And see R. A. Falk, "Appendix to Report . . ." *op. cit.*, pp. 102-103.

[151] See, for example, General Assembly Res. 95 (I), 11 Dec. 1946, by which the Assembly unanimously reaffirmed the principles of international law recognized in the Nuremberg Tribunal's Charter and judgment, and Res. 1962 (XVIII), 13 Dec. 1963, in which the Assembly unanimously declared, *inter alia*, that outer space and celestial bodies are free for exploration and use by all states in conformity with international law and are not subject to national appropriation.

107

will probably increase as a supplement to the more cumbersome treaty-making process. The actual effect of such declarations depends, of course, on several factors, including the extent to which they express a real consensus, the number and importance of the states supporting and opposing them, and the degree to which they correspond to the requirements of international life. There are many indications that the less developed nations are becoming aware of the fact that a resolution opposed by the more powerful states, or by some of them, does not carry as much weight as one that is not so opposed. The influence of the more advanced states may be expected to continue to offset, in some measure, the numerical preponderance of the less developed nations in the General Assembly, thus preventing the appearance of too large a gap between the purported content of the law and the realities of material power.

Thus, international law will continue to be "universal" in the sense that there will be a substantial number of concepts and norms understood, invoked, and followed—despite occasional violation—by all states. The scope and complexity of international law, furthermore, will continue to expand, especially in the form of treaties, in keeping with the expansion in the number and complexity of transnational activities and interactions in a shrinking world.

International law will still be viewed by many observers as inadequate and fragmentary, since it will not constitute, for a long time to come, a comprehensive order in which the most important aspects of the relations between states—including resort to violent forms of coercion—are effectively regulated by law. But legal institutions can never guarantee lasting peace and security. Even in the best organized national societies, they are often ineffective in resolving major conflicts of interest and power. In the United States, the federal Constitution and the Supreme Court did not prevent civil war a hundred years ago. The excellent British legal system did not make impossible a twentieth century civil war in Ireland. Contemporary international law, of course, is not nearly as adequate or effective as the national legal systems of well-organized states. But its role in world affairs, although not as important as the role of national law in most states, is far from negligible. In fact, it is an essential framework for many aspects of international relations, as shown by the measure of its acceptance in practice even by the Communist states.

The absolutist dichotomy between the presence and absence of world-wide agreement on values is false. In the world community, as in national societies, there is a broad spectrum of values and of degrees of consensus on them. A large measure of agreement on values does, of course, strengthen the cohesiveness of a community and the efficacy of its legal order. But it is not a question of all or nothing. A black-and-white contrast between a world in which common ideological values prevail and in which peace rests securely on law, on one hand, and a world in which lawlessness and naked force rule, on the other, is out of place here. These are but non-existent extremes of a continuum in which, as history suggests, international law will play varying roles in different periods and in relations between states with different interests and systems of public order.

Side by side with conflicting values and interests are many common or mutual interests. It is the existence of the latter that makes possible the regulation and adjustment of the conflicts of interest by law. Virtually all human beings agree on the importance of such basic material needs as survival, health, food, clothing, and shelter. Sometimes they fight over the distribution of the requisite resources, but they also often cooperate to obtain them. Conflict is virtually always intermingled in varying proportions with cooperation. Even antagonistic systems of public order such as "socialist" and "capitalist" have a common stake, for example, in the avoidance of general war, the maintenance of diplomatic relations and of facilities for international transport and communication, the conservation of certain natural resources, and the exchange of certain goods and services on a mutually advantageous basis. In the relations between the advanced and the less developed nations, the number of common or mutual interests is even greater.

As already indicated, the conflicts of interest—and particularly those caused or reinforced by the Communist ideology and system of public order—today prevent a rapid expansion of the role of law in international affairs. The more exacting demands addressed to international law are not likely to be fully satisfied in the immediate future. A world public order comparable in scope and effectiveness to the public order of a well-organized nation is still far away. In the international community there are, as yet, no formally established special institutions for orderly modification of the law and of existing legal rights without the consent of the states concerned. But the conflicts of interest do not prevent mutually acceptable regulation of transnational activities in the areas of international relations where there is some community of interest, however limited. Since all states engage in such activities, there is a basis for the existence of "universal" international law in the sense of a number of concepts and norms understood, invoked, and honored by all states, as well as of "particular" international law—norms that apply to some but not all states. Both universal and particular international law may be expected to grow in scope and complexity as the volume and variety of transnational activities increase. Universal agreement on ideological goals and ethical values is not a prerequisite for the existence—or even the growth—of international law.

BIBLIOGRAPHY

A SELECTED BIBLIOGRAPHY
OF INTERNATIONAL LAW

(In English and French)

I. GENERAL TREATISES AND RESTATEMENTS

American Law Institute, *Restatement, The Foreign Relations Law of the United States* (Philadelphia, 1965).

Cavaré, Louis, *Le Droit International Public Positif* (2 vols., Paris, Pedone, 1961).

Guggenheim, Paul, *Traité de Droit International Public* (2 vols., Geneva, Georg, 1953-1954).

Hyde, Charles Cheney, *International Law Chiefly as Interpreted and Applied by the United States* (3 vols., 2nd ed., Boston, Little, Brown, 1945).

O'Connell, D. P., *International Law* (2 vols., Dobbs Ferry, N. Y., Oceana, and London, Stevens, 1965).

Oppenheim, L., *International Law*, ed. by H. Lauterpacht (London, Longmans Green; vol. 1, 8th ed., 1955; vol. 2, 7th ed., 1952).

Research in International Law Under the Auspices of the Faculty of the Harvard Law School, *Drafts of Conventions Prepared for the Codification of International Law* (published as *Supplements* to the *American Journal or International Law*, Washington, 1929, 1932, 1935 and 1939).

Rousseau, Charles, *Droit International Public* (Paris, Sirey, 1953).

Schwarzenberger, Georg, *International Law* (vol. 1, 3rd ed., London, Stevens, 1957).

Sibert, Marcel, *Traité de Droit International Public* (2 vols., Paris, Dalloz, 1951).

II. SHORTER GENERAL WORKS, MANUALS AND CASEBOOKS

Bishop, William W., Jr., *International Law: Cases and Materials* (2nd ed., Boston and Toronto, Little, Brown, 1962).

Brierly, J. L., *The Law of Nations*, ed. by Sir Humphrey Waldock (6th ed., New York and Oxford, Oxford University Press, 1963).

Briggs, Herbert W., *The Law of Nations: Cases, Documents, Notes* (2nd ed., New York, Appleton-Century-Crofts, 1952).

Delbez, Louis, *Les Principes Généraux du Droit International Public* (3rd ed., Paris, Pichon et Durand-Auzias, 1964).

113

Gould, Wesley, L., *An Introduction to International Law* (New York, Harper, 1957).

Green, Leslie C., *International Law Through the Cases* (2nd ed., London, Stevens, and New York, Praeger, 1959).

Jessup, Philip C., *A Modern Law of Nations* (New York, Macmillan, 1948).

Kelsen, Hans, *Principles of International Law* (New York, Rinehart, 1952).

Reuter, Paul, *Droit International Public* (2nd ed., Paris, Presses Universitaires de France, 1963).

Rousseau, Charles, *Droit International Public* (3rd ed., Paris, Dalloz, 1965).

Schwarzenberger, Georg, *Manual of International Law* (2 vols., 4th ed., London, Stevens, and New York, Praeger, 1960).

Starke, J. G., *An Introduction to International Law* (5th ed., London, Butterworths, 1963).

Von Glahn, Gerhard, *Law Among Nations* (New York and London, Macmillan, 1965).

Whitaker, Urban G., Jr., *Politics and Power: A Text in International Law* (New York, Evanston and London, Harper & Row, 1964).

III. WORKS ON SPECIAL TOPICS

1. *Nature, functions, sources and history of international law*

Brierly, J. L., *The Outlook for International Law* (Oxford, Clarendon Press, 1944).

Carlston, Kenneth S., *Law and Organization in World Society* (Urbana, Ill., University of Illinois Press, 1962).

Cheng, Bin, *General Principles of Law as Applied by International Courts and Tribunals* (London, Stevens, 1953).

Corbett, Percy E., *Law in Diplomacy* (Princeton, Princeton University Press, 1959).

De Visscher, Charles, *Problèmes d'Interprétation Judiciaire en Droit International Public* (Paris, Pedone, 1963).

De Visscher, Charles, *Théories et Réalites en Droit International Public* (3rd ed., Paris, Pedone, 1960). Translation by Percy E. Corbett: *Theory and Reality in Public International Law* (Princeton, Princeton University Press, 1957).

Falk, Richard A., *The Role of Domestic Courts in the International Legal Order* (Syracuse, Syracuse University Press, 1964).

Friedmann, Wolfgang, *The Changing Structure of International Law* (New York, Columbia University Press, and London, Stevens, 1964).

Higgins, Rosalyn, *Conflict of Interests: International Law in a Divided World* (London, Bodley Head, 1965).

Higgins, Rosalyn, *The Development of International Law by Political Organs of the United Nations* (London and New York, Oxford University Press, 1963).

Jenks, C. Wilfred, *The Common Law of Mankind* (London, Stevens, and New York, Praeger, 1958).

Jenks, C. Wilfred, *The Prospects of International Adjudication* (Dobbs Ferry, N.Y., Oceana, and London, Stevens, 1964).

Jessup, Philip C., *The Use of International Law* (Ann Arbor, University of Michigan Law School, 1959).

Jessup, Philip C., *Transnational Law* (New Haven, Yale University Press, 1956).

Kaplan, Morton A., and Katzenbach, Nicholas deB., *The Political Foundations of International Law* (New York and London, John Wiley, 1961).

Kiss, Alexandre-Charles, *L'Abus de Droit en Droit International Public* (Paris, Pichon et Durand-Auzias, 1953).

Lauterpacht, H., *Private Law Sources and Analogies of International Law* (London, Longmans Green, 1927).

Lauterpacht, H., *The Development of International Law by the International Court* (London, Stevens, 1958).

Lauterpacht, H., *The Function of Law in the International Community* (Oxford, Clarendon Press, 1933).

Lipsky, George A., ed., *Law and Politics in the World Community* (Berkeley and Los Angeles, University of California Press, 1953).

McDougal, Myres S., and Associates, *Studies in World Public Order* (New Haven, Yale University Press, 1960).

Merillat, H. C. L., ed., *Legal Advisers and Foreign Affairs* (Dobbs Ferry, N. Y., Oceana, 1964).

Niemeyer, Gerhart, *Law Without Force* (Princeton, Princeton University Press, 1941).

Nussbaum, Arthur, *A Concise History of the Law of Nations* (2nd ed., New York, Macmillan, 1954).

Reuter, Paul, *Institutions Internationales* (4th ed., Paris, Presses Universitaires de France, 1963). Translation: International Institutions (London, Allen & Unwin, 1958, and New York, Praeger, 1961).

Röling, B. V. A., *International Law in an Expanded World* (Amsterdam, Djambatan, 1960).

Roulet, Jean-David, *Le Caractère Artificiel de la Théorie de l'Abus de Droit en Droit International Public* (Neuchâtel, Éditions de la Baconnière, 1958).

Schwarzenberger, Georg, *The Frontiers of International Law* (London, Stevens, 1962).

Siorat, Lucien, *Le Problème des Lacunes en Droit International* (Paris, Pichon et Durand-Auzias, 1959).

Sörensen, Max, *Les Sources du Droit International* (Copenhagen, Einar Munksgaard, 1946).

Suy, Eric, *Les Actes Juridiques Unilateraux en Droit International Public* (Paris, Pichon et Durand-Auzias, 1962).

Touscoz, Jean, *Le Principe de l'Effectivité dans l'Ordre International* (Paris, Pichon et Durand-Auzias, 1964).

Tunkin, Grigory I., *Droit International Public: Problèmes Théoriques* (Paris, Pedone, 1965).

Wolfke, Karol, *Custom in Present International Law* (Wroclaw, Polskiej Akademii Nauk, 1964).

2. *States and other entities in international law*

Charpentier, Jean, *La Reconnaissance Internationale et l'Évolution du Droit des Gens* (Paris, Pedone, 1956).

Chen, Ti-Chiang, *The International Law of Recognition* (London, Stevens, 1951).

Dickinson, Edwin D., *The Equality of States in International Law* (Cambridge, Mass., Harvard University Press, 1920).

Drost, Pieter N., *Human Rights as Legal Rights* (New York, H. H. Bentler, 1951).

Fawcett, J. E. S., *The British Commonwealth in International Law* (London, Stevens, 1963).

Feilchenfeld, Ernest H., *Public Debts and State Succession* (New York, Macmillan, 1931).

Ganji, Manouchehr, *International Protection of Human Rights* (Geneva, Droz, 1962).

Kooijmans, P. H., *The Doctrine of the Legal Equality of States* (Leyden, Sythoff, 1964).

Lauterpacht, H., *International Law and Human Rights* (London, Stevens, 1950).

Lauterpacht, H., *Recognition in International Law* (Cambridge, University Press, 1947).

Marek, Krystyna, *Identity and Continuity of States in Public International Law* (Geneva, Droz, 1954).

Nörgaard, Carl Aage, *The Position of the Individual in International Law* (Copenhagen, Ejnar Munksgaard, 1962).

O'Connell, D. P., *The Law of State Succession* (Cambridge, University Press, 1956).

Robertson, A. H., *Human Rights in Europe* (Manchester, Manchester University Press, and Dobbs Ferry, N. Y., Oceana, 1963).

Sack, A. N., *Les Éffets des Transformations des États sur Leurs Dettes Publiques* (Paris, Sirey, 1927).

Shukri, Muhammad Aziz, *The Concept of Self-Determination in the United Nations* (Damascus, Al Jadidah Press, 1965).

Vasak, Karel, *La Convention Européenne des Droits de l'Homme* (Paris, Pichon et Durand-Auzias, 1964).

Weil, Gordon Lee, *The European Convention on Human Rights* (Leyden, Sythoff, 1963).

(See also under "International Organizations")

116

3. Territory and jurisdiction
(including the law of the sea, air and space)

Barry, B. L., *The Continental Shelf* (Geneva, Droz, 1960).

Baxter, R. R., *The Law of International Waterways* (Cambridge, Mass., Harvard University Press, 1964).

Berber, F. J., *Rivers in International Law* (London, Stevens, and New York, Oceana, 1959).

Boczek, Boleslaw Adam, *Flags of Convenience* (Cambridge, Mass., Harvard University Press, 1962).

Bouchez, Leo J., *The Regime of Bays in International Law* (Leyden, Sythoff, 1964).

Brüel, Erik, *International Straits* (2 vols., London, Sweet & Maxwell, 1947).

Cheng, Bin, *The Law of International Air Transport* (London, Stevens, and New York, Oceana, 1962).

Colombos, C. J., *The International Law of the Sea* (5th ed., London, Longmans Green, 1962).

Falk, Richard A., and others, *Essays on International Jurisdiction* (Columbus, Ohio State University Press, 1961).

Ferron, Olivier de, *Le Droit International de la Mer* (2 vols., Geneva, Droz, 1958-1960).

Garcia Amador, F. V., *The Exploitation and Conservation of the Resources of the Sea* (2nd ed., Leyden, Sythoff, 1959; reprinted with Supplement, 1963).

Gidel, Gilbert, *Le Droit International Public de la Mer* (3 vols., Paris, Sirey, 1932-1934).

Hill, Norman, *Claims to Territory in International Law and Relations* (London, New York and Toronto, Oxford University Press, 1945).

Jennings, R. Y., *The Acquisition of Territory in International Law* (Manchester, Manchester University Press, and Dobbs Ferry, N. Y., Oceana, 1963).

Jessup, Philip C., *The Law of Territorial Waters and Maritime Jurisdiction* (New York, Jennings, 1927).

Jones, Stephen B., *Boundary-Making* (Washington, Carnegie Endowment for International Peace, 1945).

Lipson, Leon, and Katzenbach, Nicholas deB., *Report to the National Aeronautics and Space Administration on the Law of Outer Space* (Chicago, American Bar Foundation, 1961).

Matte, Nicolas Mateesco, *Traité de Droit Aérien-Aéronautique* (2nd ed., Paris, Pedone, 1964).

McDougal, Myres S., and Burke, William T., *The Public Order of the Oceans* (New Haven and London, Yale University Press, 1962).

McDougal, Myres S., Lasswell, Harold D., and Vlasic, Ivan A., *Law and Public Order in Space* (New Haven and London, Yale University Press, 1963).

Oda, Shigeru, *International Control of Sea Resources* (Leyden, Sythoff, 1963).

Reid, Helen Dwight, *International Servitudes in Law and Practice* (Chicago, University of Chicago Press, 1932).

Smith, H. A., *The Law and Custom of the Sea* (3rd ed., London, Stevens, 1959).

Strohl, Mitchell P., *The International Law of Bays* (The Hague, Nijhoff, 1963).

Vali, F. A., *Servitudes of International Law* (2nd ed., London, Stevens, 1958, and New York, Praeger, 1958).

4. *Immunities from jurisdiction*

Cahier, Philippe, *Le Droit Diplomatique Contemporain* (Geneva, Droz, and Paris, Minard, 1962).

Sucharitkul, Sompong, *State Immunities and Trading Activities in International Law* (London, Stevens, and New York, Praeger, 1959).

Sweeney, Joseph M., *The International Law of Sovereign Immunity* (Washington, U.S. Department of State, 1963).

Thommen, T. Kochu, *Legal Status of Government Merchant Ships in International Law* (The Hague, Nijhoff, 1962).

5. *Nationality, treatment of aliens and state responsibility*

Bar-Yaacov, Nissim, *Dual Nationality* (London, Stevens, 1961, and New York, Praeger, 1962).

Blaser, Pierre Michel, *La Nationalité et la Protection Juridique Internationale de l'Individu* (Lausanne, Nouvelle Bibliothèque de Droit et de Jurisprudence, 1962).

Borchard, Edwin M., *Diplomatic Protection of Citizens Abroad* (New York, Banks, 1915).

Dunn, Frederick S., *The Protection of Nationals* (Baltimore, Johns Hopkins Press, 1932).

Fatouros, A. A., *Government Guarantees to Foreign Investors* (New York, Columbia University Press, 1962).

Foighel, Isi, *Nationalisation* (London, Stevens, 1957).

Fouilloux, Gérard, *La Nationalisation et le Droit International Public* (Paris, Pichon et Durand-Auzias, 1962).

Freeman, Alwyn V., *The International Responsibility of States for Denial of Justice* (London, New York and Toronto, Longmans Green, 1938).

Friedman, S., *Expropriation in International Law* (London, Stevens, 1953).

Law, Castor H. P., *The Local Remedies Rule in International Law* (Geneva, Droz, and Paris, Minard, 1961).

Lillich, Richard B., and Christenson, Gordon A., *International*

Claims: Their Preparation and Presentation (Syracuse, Syracuse University Press, 1962).

Shea, Donald R., *The Calvo Clause* (Minneapolis, University of Minnesota Press, 1955).

Silvanie, Haig, *Responsibility of States for Acts of Unsuccessful Insurgent Governments* (New York, Columbia University Press, 1939).

Personnaz, Jean, *La Réparation du Préjudice en Droit International Public* (Paris, Sirey, 1938).

Van Panhuys, H. F., *The Role of Nationality in International Law* (Leyden, Sythoff, 1959).

Weis, Paul, *Nationality and Statelessness in International Law* (London, Stevens, 1956).

White, Gillian, *Nationalisation of Foreign Property* (London, Stevens, and New York, Praeger, 1961).

Whiteman, Marjorie, *Damages in International Law* (3 vols., Washington, Government Printing Office, 1937-1943).

Wortley, B. A., *Expropriation in Public International Law* (Cambridge, University Press, 1959).

6. The law of treaties

Blix, Hans, *Treaty-Making Power* (London, Stevens, and New York, Praeger, 1960).

Hendry, James McLeod, *Treaties and Federal Constitutions* (Washington, Public Affairs Press, 1955).

Hoyt, Edwin C., *The Unanimity Rule in the Revision of Treaties: A Re-examination* (The Hague, Nijhoff, 1959).

Jones, *Full Powers and Ratification* (Cambridge, University Press, 1946).

Léca, Jean, *Les Techniques de Révision des Conventions Internationales* (Paris, Pichon et Durand-Auzias, 1961).

McNair, Lord (Arnold D.), *The Law of Treaties* (Oxford, Clarendon Press, 1961).

7. Peaceful settlement of disputes

Anand, R. P., *Compulsory Jurisdiction of the International Court of Justice* (Bombay, London, and New York, Asia Publishing House, 1961).

Carlston, Kenneth S., *The Process of International Arbitration* (New York, Columbia University Press, 1946).

Delbez, Louis, *Les Principes Généraux du Contentieux International* (Paris, Pichon et Durand-Auzias, 1962).

Dubisson, Michel, *La Cour Internationale de Justice* (Paris, Pichon et Durand-Auzias, 1964).

Feller, A. H., *The Mexican Claims Commissions 1923-1934* (New York, Macmillan, 1935).

119

Hudson, Manley O., *International Tribunals: Past and Future* (Washington, Carnegie Endowment for International Peace. 1944).

Hudson, Manley O., *The Permanent Court of International Justice 1920-1942* (New York, Macmillan, 1943).

Liacouras, Peter, J., *The International Court of Justice; Materials on the Record of the International Court of Justice in Contentious Proceedings* (Prelim. ed., 2 vols., Durham, N. C., Duke University School of Law, 1962).

Lissitzyn, Oliver J., *The International Court of Justice* (New York, Carnegie Endowment for International Peace, 1951).

Rosenne, Shabtai, *International Court of Justice* (Leyden, Sythoff, 1957).

Rosenne, Shabtai, *The Law and Practice of the International Court* (Leyden, Sythoff, 1965).

Rosenne, S., *The World Court* (Dobbs Ferry, N. Y., Oceana, and Leyden, Sythoff, 1962).

Sandifer, Durward V., *Evidence Before International Tribunals* (Chicago, Foundation Press, 1939).

Simpson, J. L., and Fox, Hazel, *International Arbitration: Law and Practice* (London, Stevens, 1959).

United Nations, Secretariat, *Systematic Survey of Treaties for the Pacific Settlement of International Disputes* (Lake Success, N. Y., United Nations, 1948).

Valentine, D. G., *The Court of Justice of the European Communities* (2 vols., London, Stevens, and South Hackensack, N. J., Rothman, 1965).

8. *International organizations*

Ahluwalia, Kuljit, *The Legal Status, Privileges and Immunities of the Specialized Agencies of the United Nations and Certain Other International Organizations* (The Hague, Nijhoff, 1964).

Bowett, D. W., *The Law of International Institutions* (London, Stevens, and New York, Praeger, 1963).

Briggs, Herbert W., *The International Law Commission* (Ithaca, N. Y., Cornell University Press, 1965).

Broms, Bengt, *The Doctrine of Equality of States as Applied in International Organizations* (Helsinki, 1959).

Clark, Grenville, and Sohn, Louis B., *World Peace Through World Law* (2nd ed., Cambridge, Mass., Harvard University Press, 1960).

Detter, Ingrid, *Law Making by International Organizations* (Stockholm, P. A. Norstedt & Söner, 1965).

Jenks, C. Wilfred, *International Immunities* (London, Stevens, and New York, Oceana, 1957).

Jenks, C. Wilfred, *The Proper Law of International Organizations* (London, Stevens, and New York, Oceana, 1962).

Kasme, Badr, *La Capacité de l'Organization des Nations Unies de Conclure des Traités* (Paris, Pichon et Durand-Auzias, 1960).

Kelsen, Hans, *The Law of the United Nations* (London, Stevens, and New York, Praeger, 1950).

Kelsen, Hans, *Recent Trends in the Law of the United Nations* (London, Stevens, 1951).

Robertson, A. H., *The Law of International Institutions in Europe* (Manchester, Manchester University Press, and New York, Oceana, 1962).

Ross, Alf, *Constitution of the United Nations* (New York, Rinehart, 1950).

Seyersted, Finn, *Objective International Personality of Intergovernmental Organisations* (Copenhagen, 1963; pre-print of *Nordisk Tidsskrift for International Ret og Jus Gentium*, vol. 34 (1964), fasc. 1-2).

Sohn, Louis B., *Cases on United Nations Law* (Brooklyn, Foundation Press, 1956).

Weissberg, Guenter, *The International Status of the United Nations* (London, Stevens, and New York, Oceana, 1961).

9. Force in international law

Aroneanu, Eugène, *La Définition de l'Aggression* (Paris, Editions Internationales, 1958).

Bowett, D. W., *Self-Defense in International Law* (Manchester, Manchester University Press, 1958).

Brownlie, Ian, *International Law and the Use of Force by States* (New York and London, Oxford University Press, 1963).

Castren, Eric, *The Present Law of War and Neutrality* (Helsinki, Finnish Academy of Science and Letters, 1954).

Colbert, Evelyn Speyer, *Retaliation in International Law* (New York, King's Crown Press, 1948).

Debbasch, Odile, *L'Occupation Militaire* (Paris, Pichon et Durand-Auzias, 1962).

Draper, G. I. A. D., *The Red Cross Conventions* (London, Stevens, 1958).

Falk, Richard A., *Law, Morality and War in the Contemporary World* (New York and London, Praeger, 1963).

Flory, William E. S., *Prisoner of War* (Washington, American Council on Public Affairs, 1942).

Greenspan, Morris, *The Modern Law of Land Warfare* (Berkeley and Los Angeles, University of California Press, 1959).

Grob, Fritz, *The Relativity of War and Peace* (New Haven, Yale University Press, 1949).

Jessup, Philip C., and others, *Neutrality: Its History, Economics and Law* (4 vols., New York, Columbia University Press, 1935-1936).

Kotzsch, Lothar, *The Concept of War in Contemporary History and International Law* (Geneva, Droz, 1956).

Langer, Robert, *Seizure of Territory* (Princeton, Princeton University Press, 1947).

McDougal, Myres S., and Feliciano, Florentino P., *Law and Minimum World Public Order* (New Haven and London, Yale University Press, 1961).

Örvik, Nils, *The Decline of Neutrality 1914-1941* (Oslo, Tanum Forlag, 1953).

Pictet, Jean, *Les Conventions de Genève du 12 Aout 1959: Commentaire* (4 vols., Geneva, Comité International de la Croix Rouge, 1952-1959).

Schwarzenberger, Georg, *The Legality of Nuclear Weapons* (London, Stevens, 1958).

Singh, Nagendra, *Nuclear Weapons and International Law* (London, Stevens, 1959).

Spaight, J. M., *Air Power and War Rights* (3rd ed., London, Longmans Green, 1947).

Stanger, Roland J., ed., *Essays on Espionage and International Law* (Columbus, Ohio State University Press, 1962).

Stanger, Roland J., ed., *Essays on Intervention* (Columbus, Ohio State University Press, 1964).

Stone, Julius, *Aggression and World Order* (London, Stevens, 1958).

Stone, Julius, *Legal Controls of International Conflict* (2nd impression revised, with Supplement 1953-1958, London, Stevens, 1959).

Von Glahn, Gerhard, *The Occupation of Enemy Territory* (Minneapolis, University of Minnesota Press, 1957).

Woetzel, Robert K., *The Nuremberg Trials in International Law* (New York, Praeger, and London, Stevens, 1960).

10. *Miscellaneous*

Alexandrowicz, C. H., *World Economic Agencies: Law and Practice* (London, Stevens, and New York, Praeger, 1962).

Aroneanu, Eugène, *Le Crime Contre L'Humanité* (Paris, Dalloz, (1961).

Drost, Pieter N., *Crime of State: Penal Protection for Fundamental Freedoms of Persons and Peoples* (2 vols., Leyden, Sythoff, 1959).

Hawkins, Harry C., *Commercial Treaties and Agreements* (New York, Rinehart, 1951).

Jenks, C. Wilfred, *Law, Freedom and Welfare* (Dobbs Ferry, N. Y., Oceana, and London, Stevens, 1964).

Metzger, Stanley D., *International Law, Trade and Finance* (Dobbs Ferry, N. Y., Oceana, 1964).

Muhammad, V. A. Seyid, *The Legal Framework of World Trade* (London, Stevens, 1958).

Preiswerk, Roy, *La Protection des Investissements Privés dans les Traités Bilateraux* (Zurich, 1963).

Wilson, Robert R., *United States Commercial Treaties and International Law* (New Orleans, Hauser Press, 1960).

IV. PERIODICAL AND SERIAL PUBLICATIONS

Académie de Droit International, Recueil des Cours (The Hague; several volumes a year, lectures in English or French).

American Journal of International Law (Washington).

American Society of International Law, Proceedings (Washington).

Annuaire de l'Institut de Droit International (Basel).

Annuaire Français de Droit International (Paris).

Annuaire Suisse de Droit International — Schweizerisches Jahrbuch für Internationales Recht (Zürich; articles in French or German).

Asian-African Legal Consultative Committee, Reports of Sessions (New Delhi).

British Year Book of International Law (London).

Canadian Yearbook of International Law (Vancouver, B. C.).

Columbia Journal of Transnational Law (New York).

Egyptian Review of International Law — Revue Egyptienne de Droit International (Alexandria; some articles in English or French).

Harvard International Law Club Journal (Cambridge, Mass.).

Indian Journal of International Law (Delhi).

International and Comparative Law Quarterly (London).

International Law Association, Reports of Conferences (London, biennial).

International Organization (Boston).

Japanese Annual of International Law (Tokyo).

Journal du Droit International (Paris).

Jugoslavenska Revija za Medunarodno Pravo (Belgrade; some articles in English or French).

Nederlands Tijdsskrift voor Internationaal Recht (Leyden; some articles in English or French).

Nordisk Tidsskrift for International Ret og Jus Gentium (Copenhagen; some articles in English or French).

Philippine International Law Journal (Manila).

Revue Belge de Droit International (Belgian Review of International Law) (Brussels).

Revue de Droit International de Sciences Diplomatiques et Politiques (Geneva).

Revue de Droit International et de Droit Comparé (Brussels).

Revue Générale de Droit International Public (Paris).

Revue Hellénique de Droit International (Athens; articles in English or French).

Revue Internationale de Droit des Gens (Clermont-Ferrand).

Sovetskii Ezhegodnik Mezhdunarodnogo Prava — Soviet Yearbook of
International Law (Moscow; summaries in English).

United Nations, Yearbook of the International Law Commission
(New York).

United Nations, Juridical Yearbook (New York).

United Nations, Yearbook of Human Rights (New York).

United States, Naval War College, International Law Documents and
Studies (Washington; title varies).

Virginia Journal of International Law (Charlottesville, Va.).

Yearbook of the European Convention on Human Rights (The
Hague).

V. OFFICIAL DOCUMENTS AND OTHER SOURCE MATERIALS

1. State practice
    (a) United States
        Hackworth, Green Haywood, *Digest of International Law* (8
        vols., Washington, Government Printing Office, 1940-1944).
        Moore, John Bassett, *A Digest of International Law* (8 vols.,
        Washington, Government Printing Office, 1906).
        Whiteman, Marjorie M., *Digest of International Law* (many
        volumes, Washington, Government Printing Office, 1963-).
    (b) United Kingdom
        McNair, Lord (Arnold D.), ed., *International Law Opinions*
        (3 vols., Cambridge, University Press, 1956).
        Parry, Clive, ed., *The British Digest of International Law*
        (many volumes, London, 1965-).
        Smith, Herbert Arthur, ed., *Great Britain and the Law of
        Nations* (2 vols., London, King, 1932-1935).
    (c) France
        Kiss, Alexandre-Charles, *Repértoire de la Pratique Française
        en Matière de Droit International Public* (many volumes,
        Centre Nationale de la Recherche Scientifique, 1962-).

2. Judicial and arbitral decisions and related materials
    (a) World Court
        International Court of Justice, *Reports of Judgments, Advi-
        sory Opinions and Orders* (Leyden).
        International Court of Justice, *Pleadings, Oral Arguments,
        Documents* (The Hague).
        International Court of Justice, *Yearbook* (The Hague).
        Permanent Court of International Justice, *Publications*, Series
        A-E (Leyden).
        Hambro, E., ed., *The Case Law of the International Court*
        (3 vols., Leyden, Sythoff, 1952-1960).
        Hudson, Manley O., ed., *World Court Reports* (4 vols., Wash-

124

ington, Carnegie Endowment for International Peace, 1934-1943).

Répertoire des Décisions et des Documents de la Procédure Écrite et Orale de la Cour Permanente de Justice Internationale et de la Cour Internationale de Justice. Series 1: *Cour Permanente de Justice Internationale 1922-1945* (many volumes, Geneva, Droz, 1961-).

Syatauw, J. J. G., *Decisions of the International Court of Justice, A Digest* (Dobbs Ferry, N. Y., Oceana, and Leyden, Sythoff, 1963).

(b) Other tribunals

European Communities Court of Justice, *Recueil de la Jurisprudence de la Cour* (Luxembourg).

International Court of Justice, Registry, *Reports of International Arbitral Awards* (New York, United Nations).

International Law Reports (London; before 1950, title varied, beginning with *Annual Digest* . . .)

La Fontaine, H., *Pasicrisie Internationale* (Bern, Stämpfli, 1902).

La Pradelle, Albert de, and Politis, N., *Recueil des Arbitrages Internationaux* (3 vols., Paris, Pedone, 1905-1954).

Moore, John Bassett, *History and Digest of the International Arbitrations to Which the United States Has Been a Party* (6 vols., Washington, Government Printing Office, 1898).

Moore, John Bassett, *International Adjudications* (7 vols., New York, Oxford University Press, 1929-1936).

Parry, Clive, ed., *British International Law Cases* (many volumes, London, Stevens, and Dobbs Ferry, N. Y., Oceana, 1964-).

Scott, James Brown, *The Hague Court Reports* (2 vols., New York, Oxford University Press, 1916-1932).

Stuyt, Alexander M., *Survey of International Arbitrations 1794-1938* (The Hague, Nijhoff, 1939).

United Nations War Crimes Commission, *Law Reports of Trials of War Criminals* (15 vols., London, H. M. Stationery Office, 1947-1949).

3. National legislation

Deak, Francis, and Jessup, Philip C., eds., *A Collection of Neutrality Laws, Regulations and Treaties of Various Countries* (2 vols., Washington, Carnegie Endowment for International Peace, 1939).

United Nations, Office of Legal Affairs, United Nations Legislative Series (New York).

4. Treaties and agreements

(a) General

League of Nations, *Treaty Series* (205 vols., Geneva).

Martens, G. F. de, ed., *Nouveau Recueil Général de Traités* . . . (various series, title varies).

United Nations, *Status of Multilateral Conventions of Which the Secretary-General Acts as Depositary* (New York, looseleaf).

United Nations, *Treaty Series* (New York).

United States, Department of State, *Catalogue of Treaties 1814-1918* (reprint, Dobbs Ferry, N.Y., Oceana, 1964).

(b) Special collections

Great Britain, *Treaty Series* (London).

Hudson, Manley O., ed., *International Legislation* (9 vols., Washington, Carnegie Endowment for International Peace, 1919-1945).

Peaslee, Amos J., ed., *International Governmental Organizations: Constitutional Documents* (2 vols., 2nd ed., The Hague, Nijhoff, 1961).

Slusser, Robert M., *A Calendar of Soviet Treaties 1917-1957* (Stanford, Stanford University Press, 1959).

United States, Department of State, *Treaties in Force* (Washington, annual).

United States, Department of State, *Treaties and Other International Acts Series* (Washington, issued at irregular intervals).

United States, *Treaties and Other International Agreements* (Washington, several volumes a year).

5. Miscellaneous

Fontes Juris Gentium (Berlin, various series).

International Legal Materials (Washington, American Society of International Law).

Shiffer, Walter, comp., *Répertoire of Questions of General International Law Before the League of Nations 1920-1940* (Geneva, Geneva Research Center, 1942).

Sohn, Louis B., *Basic Documents of the United Nations* (Brooklyn, Foundation Press, 1956).

VI. BIBLIOGRAPHIES AND GUIDES

Aufricht, H., *Guide to League of Nations Publications* (New York, Columbia University Press, 1951).

Brimmer, Brenda, and others, *A Guide to the Use of United Nations Documents* (Dobbs Ferry, N.Y., Oceana, 1962).

Harvard Law School Library, *Catalog of International Law and Relations* (20 vols., Cambridge, Mass., 1965-).

Index to Foreign Legal Periodicals (London).

Index to Legal Periodicals (New York).

Selective Bibliography of the Library of the Peace Palace (3 vols., Leyden, Sythoff, 1953-1954).

INDEX

INDEX

Accretion, 14-15, 16
Afghanistan, 83
Africa, 1, 2, 44, 78, 82, 87, 92, 93, 94, 98, 103
Aggression 1, 16, 30-31, 50-51, 59, 92. See also Force.
Agreements. See Contracts; Treaties and agreements.
Aid, 83, 88, 96, 99-101, 104
Air, 21, 24, 26, 62, 67, 98, 103, 105. See also Space.
Albania, 62
Algeria, 90, 92
Aliens, 4, 25-27, 30, 43, 57, 65, 75-85, 89, 92, 103. See also Nationality; Property.
Angola, 92
Antarctica, 16, 70
Aqaba, Gulf of, 87
Arab states, 86-87. See also under names of particular states.
Arbitration, 4, 5, 26, 33, 62-63, 92, 93. See also Disputes.
Armed forces, 24
Asia, 1, 2, 51, 78, 82, 87, 92, 93, 94, 98, 103
Asian African Legal Consultative Committee 78, 90-91
Asylum, diplomatic, 6, 23
Avulsion, 14

Baltic republics, 59. See also Latvia.
Bishop, W. W., Jr., 31-32
Boundaries, 14-15, 18-20, 92. See also Territory.
Brazil, 82
British Guiana, 92
Burma, 78
Byelorussia, 10

Cambodia, 93
Cameroon, 93
Canada, 87, 88
Canals, 18, 19, 84, 92, 93
Castañeda, J., 79-80, 107
Cession, 15-17
Ceylon, 78, 83, 107
Chile, 86
China, 69, 70, 81, 83
Codification, 6, 37, 47, 73, 78, 86, 107
Colombia, 93
Colonialism. See Self-determination.
Commerce, 3-4, 5, 14, 17, 22, 25-26, 32, 46, 54, 58, 65, 90-91, 98, 99-101, 103
Communism, 2, 41, 42, 46-50, 51-54, 61-71, 72, 80, 81, 84, 102, 103, 109, 110. See also China; Europe, Eastern; Soviet Union; Yugoslavia.
Compensation. See Expropriation.
Congo, 93
Conquest, 15-16
Consensus, 4, 21, 28, 30, 35-37, 40, 57, 98, 105, 107, 108, 109
Consuls, 23-24, 54
Contiguity, 17
Contiguous zone, 20
Continental shelf, 20, 105, 106
Continuity of states, 10, 66
Contracts, 11, 17, 76
Corporations, 25, 26
Courts, 6, 22, 33, 34, 38, 40, 58, 62-63, 65-66, 90, 106. See also Arbitration; International Court of Justice; Jurisdiction; Nuremberg Tribunal; Permanent Court of International Justice.

129

Crime, 13-14, 18, 19, 20
Cuba, 13, 63, 70, 78, 83, 92
Culture, 1, 6, 70, 94-97, 102
Custom (customary international law), 34-37, 39, 56, 57, 97-98, 105-107
Cyprus, 107

Denmark, 88
Developing nations. See Less developed nations.
Diplomatic privileges and immunities. See Immunities, diplomatic.
Disarmament, 41, 52-53, 57, 67
Discrimination, 26, 42, 43, 68
Disputes, 4, 5, 6, 31-32, 33, 41, 61-63, 74, 93-94, 103. See also Arbitration.
Dominican Republic, 9

Ecuador, 86
Egypt, 44, 78, 83, 84. See also Suez; United Arab Republic.
Equality of states, 9-10, 42, 48, 50-51, 53, 91, 102
Ethiopia, 83, 93
Europe, 3, 6, 7, 15, 71, 83, 97, 98
Eastern, 51, 78, 84
European Economic Community, 98
Expatriation, 6, 25. See also Nationality.
Expropriation, 22, 26, 65, 92, 93, 94, 103. See also Property; Requisition.
Extradition, 14

Finland, 59
Fishing, 18, 20, 54, 86, 87, 88, 105
Force, 1, 2, 4, 5, 6, 8, 16, 17, 18, 19, 28, 29, 30-31, 41, 43, 44, 51, 60, 74, 77, 78, 79, 80, 81, 83, 84, 86-87, 89, 92, 102, 107, 108-109. See also Aggression.
France, 60, 70, 80

General Agreement on Tariffs and Trade, 10, 98, 103
General principles of law, 34, 37, 39, 56
Germany, 1, 9, 44, 46, 62-63, 77, 97
Goa, 92
Government, 8-11, 27. See also Continuity of states; States.
Great Britain, 6, 44, 60-61, 62, 80, 88, 93, 108
Grotius, H., 4

High Seas. See Sea.
Holy See, 38
Honduras, 93
Hot pursuit, 20
Human rights, 75, 79
Hungary, 59, 77

Iceland, 86, 88
Immunities, 22-24
armed forces, 24
consular, 23-24
diplomatic, 4, 22-23, 32, 54, 59, 60-61, 69, 107
international organizations, 24
sovereign, 22, 65-66, 90-91, 103, 105-106
Independence. See Sovereignty; States.
India, 10, 44, 75, 78, 82, 83, 92, 107
Individuals, 25-27, 31, 38-39, 67, 75
Indonesia, 78, 85, 90-91, 92
Innocent passage, 19-21
Internal (inland) waters. See Sea.
International Civil Aviation Organization, 67, 103. See also Air.
International Court of Justice, 33, 34, 36, 38, 58, 61, 62-63, 73, 93-95, 103
International Labour Organization, 62
International law
application, observance and sanctions, 4-6, 31-33, 46-54,

130

25-26, 30, 48, 50-51, 59, 85-87.
See also Air; Boundaries; Sea;
Sovereignty; Space.
abandonment and relinquishment, 16-17
acquisition, 15-17
Thailand, 93
Thalweg, 14
Trade. See Commerce.
Treaties and agreements, 4, 5, 6-7,
9, 10, 11, 12, 14, 15-21, 23, 24,
26-31, 33-37, 41-46, 48, 53-62,
65-68, 70, 73, 76, 78, 83-84, 88,
89-90, 92-94, 97-98, 102, 104,
106-108. See also Reservations.
law of, 27-30, 89, 93, 107
unequal, 42, 53, 56, 89, 93, 102
Tunkin, G. I., 49, 51, 52, 55-56
Turkey, 44

Ukraine, 10, 107
Union of Soviet Socialist Republics. See Soviet Union.

United Arab Republic, 78. See
also Egypt.
United Kingdom. See Great Britain.
United Nations, 10, 19, 30-31, 33,
35, 45, 47, 53, 61, 62, 63, 66,
73-76, 81-82, 90, 92, 93, 96, 100-
101, 103-104, 107-108. See also
International Law Commission.
United States, 6, 9, 13, 43, 44, 53,
54, 57, 60, 61, 62, 63, 68, 70, 83,
86, 87, 90, 92, 93, 108
Uti possidetis, 6

Venezuela, 92
Vietnam, 83
Vishinsky, A. Y., 49

War. See Force; Peace.
Welfare state, 95, 99
Western law, 95-97
Wilson, W., 43

Yugoslavia, 52, 69, 91